GREAT
IDEAS
for
Families
(most cost less than 99¢!)

303
GREAT
IDEAS
for
Families

(most cost less than 99¢!)

PHYLLIS PELLMAN GOOD
and
MERLE GOOD

Intercourse, PA 17534

The ideas in this book are excerpted from
a larger book originally published as *Ideas for Families.*

Design by Dawn J. Ranck

303 GREAT IDEAS FOR FAMILIES
Copyright © 1997 by Good Books, Intercourse, PA 17534
International Standard Book Number: 1-56148-211-0
Library of Congress Card Catalog Number: 96-48861

Library of Congress Cataloging-in-Publication Data
Good, Phyllis Pellman
    303 great ideas for families (most cost less than 99¢! / Phyllis
Pellman Good and Merle Good.
          p. cm.
     ISBN 1-56148-211-0
     1. Family recreation. 2. Creative activities and seat work.
I. Good, Merle . II. Title
GV182.8.G66   1997
646.7'8--dc21   96-48861
                                                          CIP

Table of Contents

Introduction

Establishing, and then maintaining, strong family life is a matter of interest and concern for many of us.

We lead lives full of demands from our jobs and careers. Sometimes we seem to have too many commitments, and we find ourselves shortchanging those we care most about. Many of us do not live close to our extended families. We feel alone in our efforts to hold things together.

This book is a collection of modest practices, natural ideas, suggestions that adapt easily—all of which can enhance the quality of a family's life together.

We gathered these ideas from many people and places. Most are simple to put into practice; few require the purchase of particular supplies or the presence of special skills.

What all the ideas have in common is a deliberateness, a conscious effort to value and cultivate family relationships and personal character.

This is a collection of actual things to do. It is not theory.

Many of the activities reflect both the way things used to be, and the way practices have changed, now that both parents work away from home in many families, now that one's social life is no longer centered around neighborhood and church, and now that outside interests compete daily for everyone's time and energy.

—Phyllis Pellman Good and
Merle Good

I.
Ordinary
Fun Times

✿ When I need a break, I fill the tub with warm water and bubbles and let the children play in the tub, while I sit in the bathroom and read or write letters. This is great when they're feeling tired and so am I.

       —Anita and Randy Landis-Eigsti, Lakewood, CO

✿ Since returning to the U.S., we often ask international students over for meals and invite them to tell us about their countries. We like to cook international foods for guests, inviting these friends and family to chop vegetables with us for Chinese egg rolls or to help us make tortillas and chapatis.

       —Richard and Jewel Showalter, Chad, Rhoda Jane, and
            Matthew, Irwin, OH

✿ We like baking bread together.

       —Ron and Betti Risser, Lancaster, PA

✿   Weird-Night-Dinners mean creating uncommon combinations or colors—purple milk, blue eggs, pink ice cream with carrot sticks. The children may choose anything in the cupboards or something that I can reasonably make. I pick the night!

—*Christine Certain, Fresno, CA*

✿   Friday evening is family night. No family member schedules an out-of-family activity without checking with the rest of us. As a four-member family, we each take our turn on one Friday night of the month to plan or be in charge of the evening's activities. In the months that have five Friday evenings, all four of us plan the evening together. The activities range from games, shopping, concerts, fairs, and anything else of interest—that is cheap!

—*Millard and Pris Garrett, Kimmi and Krissie,*
Lancaster, PA

✿   Every morning Alice and I get the day off to a fast start. We take a 20-minute hike to the mountain creek and back. Whether it's zero degrees or 70 degrees we do our daily ritual. It gives us a chance to talk if we feel like it— that usually happens on the way to the creek. On the return we might sing, pray out loud, share a scripture by memory or just meditate. You are right, we're in our early 60s and our four children are married and on their own.

Benefits? Better health, better communication, better schedule, and better togetherness! When Alice suggested this idea over four years ago after reading of another couple who did a daily walk, I wasn't all that excited. But we've found it to be a wholesome practice— physically, emotionally, and spiritually.

—*Eugene and Alice Souder, Grottoes, VA*

❁ On lovely spring and fall days (when I don't work away from home) we take a tray outside for Teatime. We make it complete with china tea cups, silver teaspoons, cloth napkins and small crackers or cookies. This is very appropriate for boys. Our son loves it!

> —*Kelli Burkholder King and John King, Jacob*
> *Hans and Suzanne Marissa, Goshen, IN*

❁ One summer the girls and their friends spent a lot of time writing a play, making the costumes, practicing together, and finally producing the play for family and friends.

> —*Ben and Lorraine Myers, Dillsburg, PA*

❁ Our daily life revolves around church, school, and lessons. Our daughter Kate loves when we do something spontaneously. Once (I can't remember when) I decided to break one of my own rules at her request (I bought a luxury item in the grocery store—without a coupon!). I just popped it into the cart and said, "Oh, why not!" Her eyes danced with delight. It was the spontaneity, not the product, which delighted her most. Of course, if we wouldn't have such frugal rules in the first place, it wouldn't be so much fun to break them!

> —*Shirley H. and Stuart W. Showalter, Goshen, IN*

❁ When we first moved to New York City the Metropolitan Museum of Art was a frequent afternoon stop. Our children were 4 1/2 and 2 1/2. Often we would only stop to visit three or four works featuring children with which our children were familiar. They included the Roman sculpture, "A Boy With a Thorn in His Foot," Goya's "Don Manuel," and Van Gogh's "First Steps."

> —*Joan and Larry Litman, Hoboken, NJ*

❀   When our oldest child was less than a year old, we began singing hymns to her at bedtime (and fussy times). We'd get the hymnal and start at the beginning and sing until she quieted. We've continued singing hymns with her through the years, and now, at age five, she knows many hymns and perks up during church when the congregation sings one of "her" songs.
    —*Tom and Sue Ruth, Lancaster, PA*

❀   Over the years we've usually read a chapter from a book after dinner. And we always read a book while traveling.
    —*Marlene and Stanley Kropf, Elkhart, IN*

❀   Because Mommy (Phyllis) loves to read more than eat (and she relishes food!), we've tried as often as possible to give her "Reading Mornings." This was especially true on Saturday mornings when the girls were younger. It was worth the effort, because Mommy was renewed after three or four hours by herself, and we all enjoyed each other more.
    —*Phyllis and Merle Good, Kate and Rebecca*
    Lancaster, PA

❀   We own quite a few postcards of famous artists' works, starting that collection in Fine Arts class in college. These cards were always stored on a table or in a cupboard within easy view and reach of our children, beginning when our eldest was quite small. They became a favorite quiet-time play, and are still available to our grandchildren.
    —*Charlotte H. Croyle, Archbold, OH*

❀   When the children return home during college breaks or from a vacation, we light a candle in their respective bedroom windows to signal an eager welcome.
   —*Ernest and Lois Hess, Lancaster, PA*

❀   When one of us parents is on a trip, we buy three post cards and send them home, one to the other parent and one to each girl—but with a twist. We lay all three cards beside each other and write our message across all three, so that those at home have to put all three cards together after they receive them in the mail. Otherwise, none of the cards makes sense.
   —*Phyllis and Merle Good, Kate and Rebecca*
   Lancaster, PA

After preschool or when I return from work, we have a Special Chat over a healthy snack. It might be only five to 10 minutes, but it helps us reconnect.
   —*Kelli Burkholder King and John King, Jacob*
   Hans and Suzanne Marissa, Goshen, IN

❀   At our house we have an Odd and Silly Box. Family members finding an odd or silly object (not intentionally made by persons) contributes to this box. Our box contains a stone shaped like a kidney bean, a malformed nut, and misshapen pretzels, to name a few. Garden vegetables such as carrots can be quite freakish, though it's impractical to add them, so they are saved as long as possible and always remembered when we check our box once each year.
   —*Lois and Randy Zook, Lancaster, PA*

2.
Specific Practices for Routine Times

❀ When the children were young, sometimes as often as once a month, we'd have a company meal, just for us. The meal was simple, but always it was elegant with a pretty tablecloth, perhaps candles, and always some of the serving dishes were family antiques. I felt that our children would care about our family things only if we used them and talked about them regularly.
—*Charlotte H. Croyle, Archbold, OH*

❀ When our children complained at mealtime about the food, we established a Grumble Box. A complainer paid a five-cent fine out of his/her allowance. It worked! On one occasion, a child was complaining about a certain dish of food. Suddenly the child remembered what he was doing and quickly exclaimed, "But that's the way I like it."
—*Omar A. and Delphia Kurtz, Morgantown, PA*

❧   My father used to prepare and serve breakfast to us high-schoolers before the rest of the family so we could catch our early bus. It was a special point of contact with him.
   —*David and Louisa Mow, Farmington, PA*

❧   Although my parents raised a large family on a limited budget, my mother found creative ways to make ordinary meals fun. One of my favorite memories involves three different types of mystery meals. In the first, everyone except my mother was banished from the kitchen, during which time she wrapped individually all items on the menu and creatively disguised them with the help of aluminum foil. She placed all wrapped food items on a pile in the center of the table. We were then instructed about the number of packages we could each choose for our meals. Whatever we each took became our meal. No finger poking and no trading of packages were allowed!
   The second type of mystery meal involved a trip to the local grocery store. Each of us (there were six) got a set sum of money to buy any food item we wished. Then, one at a time, we would go into the store and make our purchase. We could hardly contain our secret until one-by-one we would unveil our selection around the kitchen table. These meals usually consisted of all junk food (a rare treat)—from corn curls to marshmallow cookies—except for the one healthful food contributed by my mother.
   The last kind of mystery meal is the one most commonly known. It involved a menu of creative names for common foods. For example, "dirty mattress" was really an ice cream sandwich and "naughty hen mixture" was a deviled egg. Each person received a menu and then ordered their food items in four courses. The order in which one chose one's food was the order in which those items were served. Flatware and drinks also needed to be ordered.
   —*Cheryl and Jerry Wyble, Salunga, PA*

❁   When the refrigerator is full of leftovers, we list the leftovers on a piece of paper (menu). Diners order from the menu. Leftovers are much more exciting this way.
    —*Suzann Shafer Bauman, Lima, OH*

❁   We acquired some worn hymnals that we sing from before meals. The children love learning the new words and tunes and are delighted if the song is sung at church the next Sunday. We also take the hymnals when we travel in the car to pass the time. With the more familiar songs, the children like to take turns singing solos on the verses.
    —*Sue Aeschliman Groff, Kinzer, PA*

❁   We had a great method for making work a pleasure in the family in which I grew up. I am the oldest of seven children. We loved to read! When it was time for dishes, snipping beans for canning, or any other tedious task, out came one of the *Little House* books or one of the *Anne of Green Gables* books (or whatever was currently being enjoyed). One person read and the rest (Mom and the sisters) worked. Time flew!
    —*Don and Ruth Hartman, Brutus, MI*

❁   Each spring we accumulate a pile of sticks, seed pods, and fruit tree prunings on an edge of our garden. This pile becomes the fuel for the first hot dog roast of the season in late April. For young children, the love of roasting hot dogs and marshmallows is good incentive for spring clean-up work.
    —*Stan and Susan Godshall, Mt. Joy, PA*

❁   We often do crossword puzzles together, passing them to each other when we're stymied. The one in the daily paper has become a nightly ritual and keeps three of us huddled over it, sometimes until near midnight.
    —*LaVerna and Lawrence Klippenstein, Winnipeg, MB*

✿ We have tea at 10:00 p.m. daily. All other activity ceases, and we (family of four) sit around the kitchen table. While our children attended high school, they would frequently bring their friends home for tea and goodies— always at 10:00.

—*Irvin and Leona Peters, Winkler, MB*

✿ Our daughters remember joining me on warm, moonlit summer nights, lying under the stars on a specific old orange blanket in our backyard. We'd count falling stars, name constellations, tell stories, giggle, then snuggle together when it grew chilly or the mosquitoes got too thick—and put off bedtime forever.

—*Charlotte H. Croyle, Archbold, OH*

✿ Our daughters, at different ages, have asked for something to think about when they're trying to go to sleep. A few ideas: 1) 10 favorite memories with your cousins; 2) 25 words which rhyme with "sleep"; 3) name 20 streets in our city and put them in alphabetical order; 4) hum quietly a part of 12 pieces of music you enjoy (including hymns or school songs); 5) see how many persons you can name from our church who are 10 years old or younger. There are literally hundreds of fun, warm lists one can suggest.

—*Phyllis and Merle Good, Kate and Rebecca, Lancaster, PA*

✿ At our house we plan nutritious meals for every day of the week, and each person is expected to eat at least a small serving of every item. For the children that sometimes seems a monumental task. However, to offer some relief from that, Sunday evening supper is designated the "Get whatever you want" meal. It has become a fun time to search the cupboards and the refrigerator and enjoy the "no vegetables or fruits required" policy.

—*Martha and Rich Sider, Lancaster, PA*

❁   Friday evening Roger stops at a bakery on the way
home from work to pick up a special sweet treat for breakfast Saturday morning. He doesn't let anyone peek inside
and makes us guess what it is when he brings the box out
Saturday morning. We all look forward to both old favorites
and new treats.

—Roger and Pamela Rutt, Lancaster, PA

❁   Like many of today's families, we live far from other
relatives and the people we grew up with. As our daughter
grew older, we realized that she would not gain a sense of
family history unless we provided it for her. As a result, we
started telling "when I was little" stories as part of her bedtime ritual. She loved to hear about our early lives, and we
soon discovered that the stories she liked best related directly to her world as well. (After a trip to the doctor's office,
she would say "Mommy, tell me when you were little and
got sick." When she got a new trike, her daddy had to tell
about when he had a bike.)

Second, the stories didn't need to have a clear beginning, middle, and end, or a clear moral. The most popular
stories were short and described the day-to-day realities of
our childhood worlds and the ways we related to parents,
siblings, and friends ("Mommy, tell me about when you got
a new baby" was a very frequent request for the first six
months after her baby brother was born.).

Third, details about how we felt or what something
looked like or what we said always improved the story. But
woe to the storyteller who told the story again and left out a
detail or two!

Finally, my husband and I found that our own relation-
ship was enriched. By "eavesdropping" on each other's
stories we learned new things about one another.

—Susan and Scott Sernau, Sierra and Luke, South Bend, IN

❀   Dave and I each put a child to bed, and we alternate from one night to another. My own mom gave me a back rub at the end of each day and we always talked together.
—*Jenny and Dave Moser, Bluffton, OH*

❀   At bedtime at least one parent always talked and prayed with each child individually. During high school those sharing times often extended past midnight.
—*Mary and Nelson Steffy, East Petersburg, PA*

❀   A routine we have is pancakes for breakfast on Saturday mornings. In fact, as the children were learning the days of the week, Saturday was called Pancake Day more often than Saturday.
—*Daryl and Marlisa Yoder-Bontrager, Lancaster, PA*

❀   On Saturday mornings, usually throughout the school year, the kids go out with Dad to breakfast, and then get the mail and "visit" work. It gives Mom a chance to catch up after the hectic school week.
—*Mike and Kim Pellman, Matt and Brooke*
Bird-in-Hand, PA

❀   Sunday morning wake-up for the children was the sound of sacred music from the stereo.
—*Richard and Betty Pellman, Millersville, PA*

❀   Sundays we either have guests or we are guests in others' homes. When we host, the menu is chili, salad, and dessert.
—*Mary Hochstedler and Ruth Andrews, Kokomo, IN*

✿   Sunday is the day for visiting my mother, the children's grandmother. Although we live 45 minutes away, very rarely do we not visit her on Sunday. Usually my mother makes a big Italian dinner, which lasts all afternoon, during which time we recap the week's events. Sometimes I make dinner at my home and just heat it up at her house.

This weekly visit has given my children and me a sense of tradition, belonging, and long-lasting memories. It gives my mother a sense of being important in our lives and keeps her connected in a way similar to her childhood in Italy, where grandparents were always respected and loved.

—Marie Palasciano, Hazlet, NJ

✿   We like to have company for Sunday dinner—visitors or other families and friends from church. We may each invite friends, especially if our guests don't include children who are our children's ages.

—Richard and Jewel Showalter, Chad, Rhoda Jane
and Matthew, Irwin, OH

✿   Every Sunday night we have grilled cheese sandwiches, fruit salad, and popcorn for supper. If company comes, we just add or subtract some ingredients but maintain the same basic menu. I love having one day when I don't have to think about what to serve for a meal.

—Nancy and Clair Sauder, Tim and Michael, Lancaster, PA

✿   A "rule" in one of our homes was that each person at the table had to try a little of all the foods served at a meal. That practice has carried through to our present family; as a result we have children who are a delight to cook for—not sneaky eaters like many we meet today. As each of our children entered different cultures, they didn't hesitate to try strange foods.

—Jim and Dee Nussbaum, Kidron, OH

3.
Celebrating
Birthdays

❀   We wake up our birthday child with a song and lighted candles.
—*David and Louisa Mow, Farmington, PA*

❀   We always review the events of the day on which the birthday person was born: how long the labor was, when Mom, Dad, and baby went to the hospital, and other tidbits that come to mind.
—*Marian J. Bauman, Harrisonburg, VA*

❀   We kept the complete newspaper from the day each of our daughters was born. We also keep the complete newspaper from each of their birthdays through the years. When they become adults, this will be a gift to remember what was happening each year of their childhood and youth.
—*Phyllis and Merle Good, Kate and Rebecca*
    Lancaster, PA

❧   We gather together items that represent the birthday person's year. We look especially for small objects because I arrange them as a centerpiece on the table, a sort of montage of the birthday person's stage of life.

—*Allen and Roseanne Shenk family, Strasburg, PA*

❧   We have always invited both sets of grandparents to our daughters' birthday suppers. As the girls have gotten older, we've asked the grandparents to tell stories about when they were the age of the birthday person. This last year, when our older daughter turned 15, I (Phyllis) decided to be a little more deliberate about the storytelling, in an effort to bridge the generations. I wrote to each grandparent before the event and asked them to come prepared to answer three questions: What was their favorite thing to do when they were 15? What was their favorite food? What was their favorite music?

Each came with stories and, as the evening progressed, they inspired each other with more memories. Not only did we learn new things about people we thought we knew well, the evening opened new avenues of conversation for granddaughters and grandparents.

—*Merle and Phyllis Good, Lancaster, PA*

❧   On the years our children didn't have a birthday party, we invited a friend and that person's family for a birthday supper.

—*Norman and Dorothy Kreider, Harrisonburg, VA*

❧   At 10 or 11 years of age, each child spends a special weekend with the same sex parent to "prepare for adolescence." Making this a fun and exciting time provides a foundation for ongoing openness about relationships, sex, finances, education, and decision-making in general.

—*Chuck and Robyn Nordell, Fullerton, CA*

✿ Our family of young adult children gets together once a month to celebrate that month's birthdays. No birthdays that month? We get together anyway for a light evening meal.
—*John and Marilyn Burkhart, Mount Joy, PA*

✿ We wrap birthday gifts in odd shapes with newsprint or used gift wrap to save the earth. We always sing "Happy Birthday" often throughout the day, but at least once loud and off key to raise the roof.
—*David and Martha Clymer, Shirleysburg, PA*

✿ Instead of giving gifts to my nieces, we celebrate their birthdays by taking them to an ethnic restaurant, to a play, or by visiting a special place. Memories of these events outlast any gift we could give.
—*Suzann Shafer Bauman, Lima, OH*

✿ We planted a tree at my parents' farm when our son was born. We try to take a photo of him beside the tree on his birthday each year.
—*Jim and Carol Spicher and Jonathan, Mountville, PA*

✿ As each baby was born, we bought a rocking chair in which that baby would be rocked. The chair is destined to be that child's chair and will accompany him/her to college, apartments, and houses, and perhaps someday will rock his/her babies.
—*Ken and Helen Nafziger, Jeremy, Kirsten, and Zachary Harrisonburg, VA*

✿ We make a special presentation of a Bible when our children turn 12.
—*Virginia Buckwalter, Scarborough, ON*

❧   When each child turned 12, Ernie wrote a letter to the birthday person that had been years in the making.
—*Ernest and Lois Hess, Lancaster, PA*

❧   One grandmother I know has a special gift for each grandchild on his/her eleventh birthday. She takes the child on a "heritage tour" which includes a visit to her childhood home and school 25 miles from her present home. They visit a cemetery where her parents are buried, her church, and other places and people of special significance in her life. The event includes restaurant meals, an overnight, games, and individual attention.
—*Arlene Kehl, Kitchener, ON*

❧   Our church has a mentor program. At age 12 each child chooses an adult mentor, and that event is celebrated with a special ceremony in church.
—*Shirley H. and Stuart W. Showalter, Goshen, IN*

❧   To recognize the new privilege/responsibility of age 16, when the children are eligible for a driver's license, we have given them a sturdy key chain with a house key and keys for both cars. Presenting them with their own keys symbolizes the expectations and trust we have as they become more independent.
—*Stan and Susan Godshall, Mt. Joy, PA*

❧   If birthdays fall on a school day, one parent takes time off work to go to school and eat in the cafeteria with our celebrant. This is a big deal in elementary school, but may not be "cool" later on.
—*Gretchen Hostetter Maust and Robert Maust*
Adam and Amanda, Keezletown, VA

❁ I probably allowed more "messes" in the house than most parents would be willing to stand. For a birthday party one year I set up the tent (freestanding kind) in the dining room (a very large room) for a slumber party. Because the birthday was in January, the weather wasn't conducive to a camp-out. It was a spectacularly successful party. I let home-made tents or "camps" stand in the house for days until their usefulness in play diminished.

—Ann James Van Hooser, Princeton, KY

❁ Since our children no longer live with us, we miss the occasional contact with their friends. For their birthday meals at our house, we often invite several of their friends, of their choice, to dine with us. Our family is small, so we enjoy additional persons.

—Edwin and Rosanna Ranck, Christiana, PA

❁ For birthdays (and sometimes Mother's and Father's Days), we give "gift certificates" for breakfast. Most often they are from child to parent (but have been parent to child and even, occasionally, sibling to sibling!) and are "redeemed" at a local restaurant in the weeks or months following the birthday. Sometimes the "coupon" is part of a homemade birthday card; sometimes it is a separate "fash-ioned-by-the-giver" certificate or coupon. Jim and I have really treasured these outings as extra opportunity for indi-vidual times with our kids. A few times when our children were younger, these events were backpack-bicycle-trip-breakfasts to a nearby park.

—Jim and Janalee Croegaert and family, Evanston, IL

❁ One year we had each guest place a candle on the birthday cake and say something they appreciated about the birthday person.

—Ken and June Marie Weaver, Harrisonburg, VA

❧   Before our grandchildren were old enough to bake cakes for their mother (as I always did for her before she was married), I continued the tradition of baking a cake for her special day. But I let the decorating for the grandchildren to do after they arrived at our house for dinner on her special day. Peanut M&Ms and birthday candles were planted in the frosting by willing hands. It was a way I could still celebrate my daughter's birthday, yet let the children contribute, too, to the fun of celebration. (We've tried more delicate decorative candies too, but M&Ms are a favorite in spite of the fact that they make the cake look gaudy!)
   —*Ruth Naylor, Bluffton, OH*

❧   We ask if the birthday child wants friends or extended family guests at the special birthday meal. When the children were in grades one through eight, they often chose a Mystery Supper party over special foods like T-bone steak. They wanted to be surprised and eat the meal in the jumbled three-course style of a mystery supper. Here are two suggested menus for mystery suppers. The guests, of course, see only the left-hand column:

Spring Theme

Spring Thaw	— chocolate cake with ice cream
Puddles	— glass of water
Robin's Delight	— spaghetti and meat balls
Grass	— green beans
Daffodils	— roll with pats of butter
Flower Bed	— colorful jello salad
Twigs	— celery and carrot sticks
Little Dipper	— spoon
Mower	— knife
Trowel	— fork
Bugs and Slugs	— pickles and olives
Bird's Nest	— napkin and toothpick

Valentine/Lovers Theme

Lovers' Mess — tacos
Sweet and Sassy — spiced cider
Ribbons and Lace — napkin
Betwixt Two — fork
Love Sick — spoon
Peacemaker — knife
Wedding Ring — pineapple upside-down cake
Cupid's Dart — toothpick
Flaming Passion — salsa
Fragile — corn chips
Complements — refried beans and rice
Unquenchable — glass of water

—*Richard and Jewel Showalter, Chad, Rhoda Jane, and Matthew, Irwin, OH*

✿ For David's third birthday, we went with his two best "older" child friends to a museum where we have a membership and guest privileges. The next day I invited his best "little" friend and a few adult friends of ours, along with immediate family, to our house to celebrate. David was not overwhelmed trying to divide his time among lots of kids, and the adults could have relaxed conversation, too. I did not have planned activities, but simply allowed David to play with his friend and enjoy the attention and affection of all present as he felt able. It worked very well!

—*Beth A. Schlegel and David Stoverschlegel, North Wales, PA*

✿ Because both Stan and I enjoy good books, we decided to give each of the children a very special book for every birthday and Christmas. Now when they look at the row of birthday and Christmas books on their shelves, they also see a record of their changing interests over the years. We also give them a Christmas tree ornament each year so they will have their own collection when they leave home.

—*Marlene and Stanley Kropf, Elkhart, IN*

✿   Grandma gives the boys money for their birthdays, then takes them shopping so they can buy presents. She even cooperates with their "comparative shopping" wishes, and has been known to cover the entire mall and nearby stores and then retrace steps to where they found the best buy.
   —*Nancy and Clair Sauder, Tim and Michael*
   Lancaster, PA

✿   Birthdays are a time for giving "blessings." We make placemats for the special birthday person with affirmations and recognition for what she or he accomplished during the year. This includes words and pictures and a special wish for the coming year for growth. We laminate the placemats and eventually place them in a scrapbook.
   —*Mark and Leone Wagner, Lititz, PA*

✿   We adopted twin girls into our family. They were 11 months old when they came to live with us on a cold January day. Their birthday is in February, and the adoption became final in September, 18 months later. We celebrate all three events, with the birthday being the biggest event for them, and "Homecoming," or the day they came to live with us, being the most memorable for the rest of the family. Adoption day is important but is usually low-key because it was anticlimactic for us as a family, and sometimes we almost forget it.
   We usually have cakes and some kind of gift. Homecoming Day is a private event with just family. We tell about our going to get them and bringing them home, complete with pictures of the event which replace infant pictures for us. Most often the birthday is shared with friends as well as family, sometimes with a party, or an event such as ice or roller skating, or a sleep-over with a few friends.
   —*Karen Martin, Evanston, IL*

4.
Advent
and Christmas

✿ About 30 days before Christmas, we hang a red, white, and green paper chain with 30 links. The children take turns removing a link each day.

—*Mr. and Mrs. Nelson Schwartzentruber, Lowville, NY*

✿ When our children were young, we set up the stable under the tree. Everything was there but Mary, Joseph, and Jesus. They traveled from room to room (or wherever the boys would move them) until Christmas morning when they arrived at the stable.

—*Hazel Miller, Hudson, IL*

✿ Each Christmas Eve our children bring their sleeping bags and snacks, spend the night (it's quite a "spread" on our basement floor!), and stay for Christmas brunch together. Most everyone has another family get-together to go to after that.

—*John and Marilyn Burkhart, Mount Joy, PA*

✿   We have had an Advent calendar and "wreath" (really just four candles with a small wood carving of Mary and Jesus as a child placed in the center), partly to give the children a bit more understanding and an opportunity to ask questions about what we've done at church during the Advent candle-lighting. Church practices can be special in a certain way, but can sometimes lose something due to the lack of a two-way conversation.

   —*Allen and Roseanne Shenk family, Strasburg, PA*

✿   During Advent we invite a different family each year to come share a shepherd's supper with us. We instruct the guests to come dressed as shepherds and shepherdesses. We light our home with candle or lantern light. We eat what the shepherds may have eaten—black bread, cheese, figs, dates, venison stew, and fruit. If the guests have free imaginations, we sometimes each assume the role of a character from the Christmas story and talk together in that way over the meal. Some families have their imaginations stretched simply by coming as shepherds. We accept that and remember we are sharing joy and the story which we read together at the close of the meal.

   —*David and Martha Clymer, Shirleysburg, PA*

✿   As a couple, we have established a Christmas Eve tradition that has become meaningful to us. In the late afternoon on Christmas Eve, we begin a pre-set round of holiday visits to elderly relatives who are either childless or single. We take along a simple gift, such as a red rose for each person or a fruit tray. Our visit at each home is short, lasting only 45 minutes to an hour before we move on to the next home. Our elderly relatives have come to expect us. This tradition has filled what would otherwise be a quiet and lonely evening for all of us with much love and laughter.

   —*Cheryl and Jerry Wyble, Salunga, PA*

❁ At sundown on Christmas Eve, we go as a family to give a small gift to each of our surrounding neighbors. It has become so traditional that we sit and talk, spending much of the evening catching up with how life is going for each of those families. At 11:00 p.m. on Christmas Eve we attend a Christmas Eve service, always choosing a different place each year.

> —*Millard and Pris Garrett, Kimmi and Krissie*
> *Lancaster, PA*

❁ When our boys were little, we often walked through our neighborhood on Christmas Eve to work off some energy and to admire the decorations. When we got back home we would have a special dessert, often ice cream in holiday shapes.

> —*Nancy and Clair Sauder, Tim and Michael*
> *Lancaster, PA*

❁ We celebrate St. Nicholas Day on December 6 and focus the Santa story there. The gifts we exchange on December 24 and 25 are gifts to remember the Christ child who comes into our world. We have a birthday party for Jesus, with cake and candles on December 25.

> —*Beth A. Schlegel and David Stoverschlegel*
> *North Wales, PA*

❁ The children are grown and gone from home, but we have preserved a tradition we began when they were growing up. At our family gathering, we recite in unison and, as much as possible, by memory, the Christmas story as found in Luke 2. To ensure their rehearsing this before our gathering we send out typed copies of Luke 2 to each household and encourage them to memorize it.

> —*Marie K. Wiens, Hillsboro, KS*

❀   Make a Christmas wreath. Decorate it with little orna-
ments your children make which are symbols of Christmas
(star, camels, dried figs, manger herbs). Place it on your
front door. When guests come during the holiday season,
give them one item per household from the wreath as a
reminder of what Christmas really means. This will initiate
wonderful discussion of the true meaning of Christmas in
your household and will help your children articulate their
beliefs to others.
    —*Nancy Nussbaum, Elkhart, IN*

❀   My grandparents entertained foreign students and foreign army officers in their home for years. Christmas was
always an international affair for my family. Occasionally a
foreign student would cook an international dish for us.
None of us had ever traveled overseas, yet we knew people
from many different countries around the world.
    —*Dawn J. Ranck, Strasburg, PA*

❀   Now that our children are married, they come to our
home with their spouses and children for a Christmas Eve
supper. They all spend the night and we have Christmas
Day together, sharing in providing meals. Every other year
they spend Christmas Day with their spouses' families, so on
those years we choose another date for our overnight and
next-day gathering to celebrate Christmas.
    —*Richard and Betty Pellman, Millersville, PA*

✿ In November we select a date when the whole family can go look for a tree. We also choose a date when the tree will be decorated (generally the first or second Sunday in December). Everyone participates in these days. They take precedence over all other schedule requests which come up.

—*Jane-Ellen and Gerry Grunau, Winnipeg, MB*

✿ We are now taking our grandchildren along to choose a Christmas tree at a tree farm early in November and to cut it early in December. It's not quite the same as going to one's own pasture or woods, but it is a meaningful time, nonetheless.

—*Paul and Elaine Jantzen, Hillsboro, KS*

✿ Keith's family is scattered around the country. But at Christmastime we all gather for at least a week at Grandma and Grandpa's house. We all have our own rooms for our families to sleep in. The grandchildren love it. The meals are shared, each family taking turns in the kitchen. Each day we prepare a brunch and then an early supper with snacks available anytime.

The biggest priority of the week is "share time." One evening after all the children are sleeping, or on an afternoon during naptimes for the little ones, the adults gather in a circle. Each couple or single adult shares what is new for them, or a specific prayer concern. We try to limit ourselves to 15 minutes each. After everyone shares we spend time in prayer for each other.

—*Keith and Brenda Blank, Rebekah, Laura, and Matthew*
     Philadelphia, PA

✿ At Christmas we make cookies and deliver them to the local fire and police departments. We thank them for their service to us and tell them that we pray for them regularly.

—*Chuck and Robyn Nordell, Fullerton, CA*

❁   During Christmas Eve night, we lay an unwrapped gift on the foot of each child's bed—something to keep them occupied in the early hours before they may waken us!
   —Phil and Sandy Chabot, Becky and PV, Cromwell, CT

❁   A tradition we began, upon receiving a jigsaw puzzle for Christmas one year, is to complete a puzzle the week between Christmas and New Year. It becomes the beginning of our puzzle craze during the winter months that follow! Younger children can help sort borders and colored pieces. When the puzzle comes to the difficult parts and the children no longer feel included, we work on the puzzle after the children are tucked into bed!
   —Lois and Randy Zook, Lancaster, PA

❁   A friend of mine always saves one Christmas gift for each family member to open on Epiphany. It helps with the post-Christmas letdown.
   —Elizabeth Weaver, Thorndale, ON

❁   The month of January is our favorite time to make our gingerbread house. It offers something to look forward to after the Christmas rush.
   —Lois and Randy Zook, Lancaster, PA

5.
Seasons
and Milestones

❀   I (Betty) like to send cards for special times and decorate the envelopes to either fit the occasion or the child's interest. I also like to wrap our family gifts in brown bags and then decorate them with drawings. It adds a special touch for the giver and the receiver.
   —*Richard and Betty Pellman, Millersville, PA*

❀   A couple of weeks before Easter, I plant grass seed in Andrew's Easter basket so that by Easter there's "real grass" in his basket. He enjoys watching the grass grow and anticipates the arrival of Easter.
   —*Ron and Betti Risser, Lancaster, PA*

❀   For many years anyone in the family who wanted could go for a walk on Easter morning at sunrise with Dad. Often one or more of the kids went, while the rest stayed to help with dinner preparations.
   —*Jim and Dee Nussbaum, Kidron, OH*

❀ We share Maundy Thursday or Good Friday with another family from our church. Children and adults eat a meal together and then read the Passion story from the Bible. Each person holds a candle, and lighting is done symbolically as we read the story. This small celebration together makes our Easter service at church on Sunday morning a more special time.
*—Kenny and Rachel Pellman, Nathaniel and Jesse
Lancaster, PA*

❀ Coloring, hiding, and hunting Easter eggs is such fun, but we didn't like it detracting from the meaning of Jesus' resurrection on Easter Sunday, so we found an alternative. On Palm Sunday we invite several families to join us for a potluck, bringing with them some eggs they have colored, as well as some plastic eggs filled with surprises. After lunch and an egg hunt for the children, the adults each hunt a plastic egg that was hidden for them. Prior to hiding these eggs, each adult made a coupon for something that they would do for another, then placed these coupons in the eggs to be hidden. Coupons include such things as one car wash and cleaning, a loaf of freshly baked bread, three hours of babysitting, two hours of window-washing or yard-mowing, etc.
—Herb and Sarah Myers and daughters, Mount Joy, PA

❀ At Eastertime Mom and the children make peanut butter eggs to give as gifts to teachers, family, and friends.
*—Mike and Kim Pellman, Matt and Brooke
Bird-in-Hand, PA*

❀ At Easter as our children were growing up, we usually colored eggs with another family and had great fun together.
—Arlene S. Longenecker, Oxford, PA

✿ We've had an Easter tradition of hiding and hunting Easter baskets. To lessen sugar consumption for our grandchildren, we replaced candy in the Easter baskets with T-shirts when the children were younger, and more recently with other gifts or money, also hidden and waiting to be found.

—*Richard and Betty Pellman, Millersville, PA*

✿ "Don't beg for things," we tell our children, but one night a year we disguise them and send them out to collect as much loot as possible. When we were children, we were forbidden to go halloweening, but we were given no alternatives. We have experimented with and enjoyed several other ideas which have come to be known and celebrated as our Alternative Halloween. We invite two or three other families and/or singles to join us for an evening of fun. We bob for apples, eat powdery homemade doughnuts dangling from a string, and play Bible Charades. The climax of the evening for the children comes when the adults hide somewhere in the house. Upon finding one of the adults, the children receive a piece of candy or some other small nonedible treat. The hunt continues till each child has as many treats in his or her bag as there are hidden adults.

—*Herb and Sarah Myers and daughters, Mount Joy, PA*

✿ In Oregon we always eagerly anticipated the June strawberry harvest. Each year we went to the fields to pick our own berries (even taking the children along in backpacks when they were very small). Then came the best part—a meal of strawberry shortcake with plate-sized biscuit-type shortcake, heaps of fresh strawberries, and sweet cream. Even after we moved to Indiana we continued our tradition of the strawberry shortcake meal.

—*Marlene and Stanley Kropf, Elkhart, IN*

❀ When our older daughter was preparing for baptism, we asked each other why the biggest celebrations families traditionally give their children are graduation parties and/or wedding receptions. Doesn't a child's faith decision and entry into the church merit a celebration? (Besides, they may never marry or graduate.)

And so we had a celebration for each daughter on the evenings before their baptisms. We invited grandparents, aunts, uncles, and cousins, our pastor, and a few friends from church. We began with a get-acquainted quiz (guests had to recall details from their own baptisms) and followed that with a feast, lots of visiting, and, finally, singing, inviting everyone to offer their choices from the hymnal. We decorated the house with flowers and balloons and asked two uncles to take photos throughout the events.

Then we provided each daughter with a photo album for her to fill with her choice of pictures from her party. The solemn occasion took on real joy and a swell of support from each child's closest acquaintances.

—Merle and Phyllis Good, Lancaster, PA

❀ Our favorite Special-Seasons tradition is an annual wildflower trip (sometimes two or three a season) to West Virginia mountain areas, backroads, and woods to find rare flowering plants. Each fall we have "color trips," again to mountain areas with picnics, walks, and photo-taking times.

—Shirley Kirkwood, Mt. Solon, VA

❀ Since Mother's Day usually falls during morel mushroom season, my traditional Mother's Day breakfast is a morel omelette.

—Tom and Lois Marshall, Naomi, Christine, and Jonathan, Spruce, MI

❀ Phyllis, Kate, and Rebecca were in a very serious accident several years ago. A drunk driver hit our car head-on one Friday morning when the three of them were shopping. All three were taken to the emergency room and admitted. It was very traumatic for all of us. Rebecca was released on the second day and Phyllis on the third. But Kate had compressed vertebrae in her back and a messed-up jaw. Two weeks later she came home to a hospital bed in which she lay for another month.

All three are now fully recovered. And as an annual ritual of gratefulness and celebration, we return to the hospital for a meal in their cafeteria. We reminisce, and the girls are permitted unlimited desserts. It's a fun way to keep processing a near tragedy.

—Phyllis and Merle Good, Kate and Rebecca, Lancaster, PA

❀ When the men in our extended family are at the mountains hunting for deer in November, the women and children get together to make graham cracker houses. The oldest grandchildren are now 13, and they still look forward to it.

—Jay and Linda Ebersole, Rosalyn, Randy, and Ryan,
Lancaster, PA

❀ On one of our wedding anniversaries our four children gave us a scrapbook that they had made and gathered. They gave blank pages to their aunts, uncles, and neighbors and had them fill both sides with pictures, special memories, or anything they wanted to put on it. We were given 100 pages of pictures and memories, a gift we will long treasure.

—Janet Roggie, Lowville, NY

❀ The last day of school is usually a half day, so we go out for lunch to celebrate.

—Nancy and Clair Sauder, Tim and Michael
Lancaster, PA

✿   We have a School's Out Party. We cook the children's favorite foods for dinner, watch a video together, or play games and stay up late! We all sleep in one room in sleeping bags.
—Wayne and Mary Nitzsche, Wooster, OH

✿   We have a tradition of "report card meals." Regardless of the grades, we go out twice a year to celebrate the milestone of finishing another half year of school. The girls take turns choosing the restaurant (within reason).
—Phyllis and Merle Good, Kate and Rebecca, Lancaster, PA

✿   The children's mother died of cancer, and on the anniversary of her death, my husband recounts the events of her illness and death for the children, to keep her memory alive.
—Marian J. Bauman, Harrisonburg, VA

✿   We have experienced several miscarriages. We've planted some perennial flowers as a way to mark that loss and to remind us annually of God's gift of life.
—Jim and Carol Spicher, Jonathan, Mountville, PA

✿   On the July 6 anniversary of our 12-year-old Bruce's death, we talk about him and do something he would have enjoyed, like make a trip to the Dairyette or hike at the Wilderness Center, a camp used for sixth grade outdoor education.
—Clayton and Ruth Steiner, Dalton, OH

✿   As we left one home for another, we loaded our memory banks by going from room to room, and from the garden to other favorite outdoor spots, soaking up all the wonderful associations with each.
—Ernest and Lois Hess, Lancaster, PA

6.
Extended Family
and Friends

❁   LETTERS! LETTERS! LETTERS! Phone calls are quick, easy, and, at off hours, not overly expensive. But what do you have to show for them after the phone clicks?

Letters last. They can be read and reread, savored and saved. Years later they bring back many memories. Sunday afternoon each week we write to our parents.

—*Herb and Sarah Myers and daughters, Mount Joy, PA*

❁   My husband and I do not have children at the present time. Sometimes we feel quite lonely and "childless." I've heard things like: "Oh, we can't come over for lunch after church because the little one needs a nap and you don't have a crib." So——guess what we bought for five dollars at an auction? Yep! I now preface invitations to our home for Sunday afternoon with: "We have a crib if _____ needs to nap."

—*Nancy Nussbaum, Elkhart, IN*

✿   Over the years we often babysat nieces and nephews for weekends. This gave their parents some time on their own, allowed us to learn to know the children better, and provided playmates for our boys. When our boys were teenagers and the visiting nieces and nephews were pre-schoolers, it added an interesting dimension to our family life.
        —*Arlene Kehl, Kitchener, ON*

✿   Our son's favorite uncle took an assignment overseas for three years. To help him remember this special uncle, we began compiling a scrapbook just about this person. In it we arrange photos, articles about him, his art and letters, and anything else which seems relevant to the child.
        —*Kelli Burkholder and John King, Goshen, IN*

✿   Since Bonita's mother has Alzheimers, Bonita takes care of her at our house one day a week. On those evenings, we have both her mother and father for supper if they care to stay. It has been a way for our children to observe aging and caring. We have also grown much closer to Bonita's parents.
        —*Ervin and Bonita Stutzman, Mount Joy, PA*

✿   Family reunions don't happen after the parents are gone, unless one makes a plan to continue to come together. We are widely scattered, so we have a reunion every five years. T-shirts with our family name are a popular item for such occasions.
        —*Marie K. Wiens, Hillsboro, KS*

✿   The girls' grandparents planted a tree for each grandchild in the lot behind their house. Our girls enjoyed helping to plant the tree (when they were three or four), and it gives them a sense of owning part of Grandpa's and Grandma's place!
        —*Phyllis and Merle Good, Kate and Rebecca, Lancaster, PA*

✿   We try to spend every other Friday with my parents, helping with household jobs and taking time to learn from each other. My dad's interest in genealogy gives me much information and lots of stories of his past. Mom and I are learning that life's experiences help us to be more and more alike!

> —*Millard and Pris Garrett, Kimmi and Krissie*
> *Lancaster, PA*

✿   We sometimes invite single and married friends for a music evening or poetry time. Presently we're in the process of having each single person from our congregation over for a meal.

> —*LaVerna and Lawrence Klippenstein, Winnipeg, MB*

✿   My husband invites international students to hike with him, and we have them in for meals and evenings.

> —*Shirley Kirkwood, Mt. Solon, VA*

✿   For over 15 years we introduced our family to other nationalities and cultures by entertaining Fresh Air children from New York City. Over the years we also entertained some 40 international students—a good experience for all ages.

> —*Omar A. and Delphia Kurtz, Morgantown, PA*

✿   When the children were very small, we organized an exchange with four families for Monday nights. One set of parents kept all seven children and planned a special project for them. The other three sets of parents were free to do something together or alone every Monday evening from 7:00 to 10:00. The children developed special relationships, as well as all parents with each other's children.

> —*Linda and Ron Gunden, Lisa and Angela, Elkhart, IN*

❀   We have adopted an annual tradition with another family. When our children were young, we would see people around us packing up their families and heading down to a nearby city for a long weekend by the pool. Our two families felt we could not afford this, nor did we see much benefit in stuffing our six children into two small hotel rooms, so we planned a "big city" weekend in another part of our own home town!

Our friends moved into our home for the weekend, and we settled into theirs. We did not answer the phone. We cancelled all our commitments. We spent the weekend swimming, tobogganing, renting a movie, playing games, etc. Our meals were simple. We had such a good time that we have, with a few exceptions, continued this practice every year. It has become a little more difficult to cancel all commitments as the children have gotten older, but we all enjoy the weekends.

—*Jane-Ellen and Gerry Grunau, Winnipeg, MB*

❀   A fun activity to do with guests (especially an inter-generational group) is to divide them into groups of three or four, mixing the ages, and giving them all the same word to pantomime. Each group heads to private corners throughout the house to plan their presentation. Then each returns and acts out their wordless "drama," while the rest try to guess how they are using the word they've all been given. (Words like "star," "peace," and "spring" allow a lot of imagination to be expressed.)

—*Merle and Phyllis Good, Kate and Rebecca*
Lancaster, PA

❁   We like to follow our summer backyard picnics with a downtown scavenger hunt. We've found it a way to introduce guests to the city's loveliness, its architectural secrets, its history. We split up into two teams and give each a list of questions to answer. (The questions are the same for both teams, but they are listed in reverse order, so that each group follows its own route, but passes the other team at midpoint.) The idea is to answer all questions correctly and be the first team to return to our house. It's good exercise, it's gently educational, it's possible for inter-generational groups, and it's worn away some skeptics' prejudices about living in the city.
> —*Merle and Phyllis Good, Kate and Rebecca*
> *Lancaster, PA*

❁   We have begun inviting our local friends (especially friends with children who usually need to leave early in the evening to get their children to bed) to stay overnight so we can have good conversation after the children go to sleep. Usually we get together on a Friday night for supper and are together through brunch on Saturday, either made at home or eaten in a family restaurant. We (parents) feel a lot more satisfied with the amount and quality of time we have with our adult friends, and the children enjoy the excitement of a sleep-over, as they share their rooms with our guests.
> —*Mary Alice and Gerald Ressler, Lititz, PA*

❁   We're all busy, and with school activities and homework, we don't visit grandparents as much as we'd like to. One partial solution occasionally is to meet at a restaurant for supper. No one has to cook, clean, or miss an evening meeting at church or elsewhere. We can sit and visit for an hour or two and still get home in time to finish homework.
> —*Phyllis and Merle Good, Kate and Rebecca*
> *Lancaster, PA*

❀   For our parents' 75th and 80th birthdays we've had family gatherings or dinners which included slide presentations chronicling theirs and their families' lives during the previous 25-30 years. The grandchildren especially enjoyed this activity—noting the changes in their relatives.

For our parents' 50th wedding anniversary our families planned an open house and family dinner. In addition, we gave them a photo album in which each of their children had filled several pages. These included photos of their family involved in activities they enjoyed and often included the grandparents with their grandchildren.

My husband's mother has made many quilts over the years. Each of her children received several when they were married, and she has also given one or more to each of her 19 grandchildren. For her 86th birthday we presented her with a photo album showing a current picture of each of her grandchildren with his/her quilt, plus her children with one of their quilts. On the cover of the album was a cross-stitched picture with the words, "Those who sleep under a quilt sleep under a blanket of love."

—*Arlene Kehl, Kitchener, ON*

❀   Some enjoyable times that our family has had with extended family have been our trips to the places where the grandparents (our parents) grew up. We take the better part of a day, charter a vehicle, visit the home, the school, and other important sites of that grandparent's childhood and youth. Children are involved with their cousins in experiencing the sights, smells, and sounds—we often provide a quiz for the kids. And we foster storytelling by the grandparents, including a sister or brother of theirs who can help flesh out the stories. Old memories create new memories.

—*Phyllis and Merle Good, Kate and Rebecca*
   Lancaster, PA

❖ Our family now lives on both coasts and in the Midwest and Canada. The cousins don't have many opportunities to learn to know each other, so I (Grandma) collect family member photos, and on their birthdays I send each grand-child a few pages to add to her/his "Birthday Book." This keeps the cousins all current on each other's activities and progress.

—*Helen G. Kennell, Eureka, IL*

❖ Keith's family has had a circle letter for at least 12 years. (There are seven families, living in various states/countries.) We each write no more than one full page and must send it off to the next household within three days of receiving it. By the time it gets around to us again, about one to one-and-a-half months have passed. Before we send our next letter, we take out our old one and file it. This col-lection will be a wonderful diary for our own family in the future.

—*Keith and Brenda Blank, Rebekah, Laura, and Matthew Philadelphia, PA*

❖ We only see some of our family once a year. I keep updated pictures of our children's cousins close by in small photo albums. We talk about these cousins quite often. I have our daughter draw pictures and send them in the mail to these extended family members.

—*Brenda Augsburger Yoder, Lancaster, PA*

❖ We have created traditions around visits with my nieces. One favorite tradition is the Cousins' Meal. The meal is prepared by the four cousins with some help from me. The complexity of the meal has increased as the cousins have matured. We started with French bread pizza and have progressed to lasagna, salad, and brownies.

—*Suzann Shafer Bauman, Lima, OH*

✿   My husband and his two brothers (ages 74, 67, and 58) have breakfast together every Thursday morning at 6:00 a.m. And we have an "aunts and cousins" luncheon once each year.
—*Iona S. Weaver, Lansdale, PA*

✿   Almost all our get-togethers are potlucks so the work load is shared.
—*Miki and Tim Hill, Woodstock, MD*

✿   Five years ago we formed a dinner group with three other households. The group provides fellowship, stimulating dinner conversation, and an opportunity for our children to interact regularly with other adults. It also relieves the burden of meal preparation. It is understood that meals are to be simple (often soup, salad, and bread). The setting is very informal. The soup pot goes directly from the stove to the table. There are not expectations to remain beyond the 6:00-7:00 dinner time. People often "eat and run."

We meet for dinner two evenings each week, rotating among the four households. When we meet at our house, we are responsible for meal preparation and cleanup. The others simply come and relax. The other three evenings we're the ones to just go and relax. We've maintained our commitment to this type of a small group longer than any other because it doesn't require extra time (we would eat meals anyway), and it involves our whole family.
—*Martha and Rich Sider, Lancaster, PA*

✿   All of our extended family lives at least 3,000 miles away from us. Holidays are times when we include singles, internationals, and other families "in orbit." It's a different group every time.
—*Joan and Larry Litman, Hoboken, NJ*

✿   We used to have an "extended family meal" each Thursday evening. It was a special meal, and we always included a nearby aunt, a nearby single woman from church, and, sometimes, "visitors." We experimented with different foods and eating styles, and "our extras" often had great ideas and helped provide food. We found it worked best before our kids reached the teen years and became super busy.

—*Bylers, Williamsport, PA*

✿   Although we have no children of our own, children seem to enjoy coming to our home. I started a tradition when children come for a meal. I put a white sheet on the table (as a tablecloth) and have several boxes of fabric crayons on hand. Each child is invited to make a beautiful work of art on the sheet. Their parents help them write their names and the date. Each time they come, the children look to see not only where their pictures are, but who else has been to our home since their last visit! This gives children something to do while they are waiting for the last-minute preparations (or after the meal) and also gives them a strong message that they are important in our lives.

This technique works with regular crayons, too. You simply need to put a paper bag between a hot iron and the drawing for a few seconds to fuse the crayon into the fabric before washing. It makes a lovely tablecloth which I will cherish for years to come!

—*Nancy Nussbaum, Elkhart, IN*

✿   Each year Grandma filled an Easter plate for each grandchild. We returned the plate to Grandma before the next Easter for a refill. Years later, we fill these same plates for our grandchildren, who return them to us for the annual refill.

—*Edwin and Rosanna Ranck, Christiana, PA*

7.
Giving Individual Attention

✿   On birthdays Grandma and Grandpa Roth take each child (alone) out to eat. These grandparents live out-of-state but always manage to set a time close to the special day. It's an event our children look forward to, even if it's a month after their birthdays!

On birthdays Grandma Miller bakes a homemade pie for each of her 23 grandchildren (and eight children), and the birthday person chooses the kind. She, too, lives out-of-state but always manages to get the pie to the birthday person, at least close to the day. Whenever it arrives, early or late, it's always a treat!

—*John and Ruth Miller Roth, Sarah, Leah, Hannah and Mary, Goshen, IN*

✿   When our children were between two and six years old, I went grocery shopping in the evening and took only one child with me at a time. They loved the attention and I expected them to help me find the groceries.

—*Marvin and Rachel Miller, Indianapolis, IN*

✿   When our children were small, we took each one sepa-
rately to a symphony concert. Now I am having each grandchild come for a day and overnight. Just the two of us do
something special, like take a train ride or go to the
"hands-on-house" or a museum or doll store, and then have
lunch at the restaurant of his or her choice.
            —*Arlene S. Longenecker, Oxford, PA*

✿   My husband takes one daughter at a time with him when
he goes for machinery parts or visits the local grain elevator.
Both girls have adult friends I've never met. Dave takes advan-
tage of these drives by having some interesting talks with our
six-year-old. And, the girls are learning about farming.
            —*Jenny and Dave Moser, Bluffton, OH*

✿   When the children came home from school, I tried to
have a snack ready or easily available, and made time to sit
down and talk. When they got home at different times, it was
easier to manage. I tried to get to know each of their teachers
and many of their classmates and families in elementary
school. I also was available to talk when they went to bed.
            —*Phyllis Eller, La Verne, CA*

✿   Our daughter has three girls; two are twins. To avoid
competition she looks for activities in which each child can
excel. One is taking piano lessons, another violin lessons,
and another aerobic exercise.
            —*H. Howard and Miriam Witmer, Manheim, PA*

✿   Our children were assigned turns to help with evening
dishes with a parent. While closely working together with
one of us, the child shared his/her day's experiences and
concerns. For this reason, our getting a dishwasher was
delayed for many years.
            —*Marvin and Violet Jantzi, Medina, NY*

❧   For each of our three children I have made complete photo albums from their births to the present. I write the dates and events on the back of each photo, then place them in albums chronologically, so that each photo can be easily removed to see the writing on back and then replaced. The children love to look at their personal albums and each other's. Because of the cost and time invested in these, I keep them on a high shelf in a closet where they can be gotten down only with adult assistance. This serves two purposes: (1) to protect them, with some adult supervision; (2) they're "out of sight, out of mind" so the children don't think about them as readily as their things that they can see and reach. If the children are bored, I periodically suggest getting their photo albums down, and that's always a big hit.
   —*Pamela and Roger Rutt, Lancaster, PA*

❧   I took "first day of school" pictures every year of each of our daughters. What a record to look at, from a very worried kindergartner to a confident senior in high school!
   —*Clive and Margaret LeMasurier, Plainville, CT*

❧   Driving time is one of the best settings for talking— forced togetherness, no danger of a sibling overhearing, and you don't have to look at each other!
   —*Lois and Jim Kaufmann, New Paris, IN*

❧   On occasion when we're driving here or there, one of us parents rides in the back seat with one of the girls while the other daughter rides up front beside the driver. The conversation in the car is remarkably different, often happier.
   —*Phyllis and Merle Good, Kate and Rebecca Lancaster, PA*

✿   We have monthly date night. My husband and I each take one child out for a date. (We also have a "date night budget" which they know about or else it could get quite expensive!) We have the best time on our dates because we are out as friends, giving one-on-one attention. We've been doing this since the kids were about five and eight. I also try to have a semi-regular "child of the day" once or twice a month. That child chooses dinner, gets served first, says the blessing, and is just made to feel extra special.
          —*Patrick and Gina Glennon, Turnersville, NJ*

✿   If birthdays fall on a school day, one parent takes time off work to go to school and eat in the cafeteria with our celebrant. This is a big deal in elementary school, but may not be "cool" later on.
          —*Gretchen Hostetter Maust and Robert Maust*
          Adam and Amanda, Keezletown, VA

✿   Even though we're a small family, we've sensed a need to spend some stretches of time alone with each child. We instituted One-on-One Days soon after both girls began school and we had less time at home with them.
On a One-on-One Day, each parent takes one child on a special excursion, planned in secret by just the two of them. (These have been mostly to local destinations, although a few times we've gone to some nearby cities to a special art show or attraction.) The emphasis is on doing what the child enjoys and having plenty of time to visit together. Then we all meet for supper together at a prearranged time and place to disclose to each other what we did for the day. Our modest goal has been to have at least two One-on-One Days each year (often in the summer) so that each parent and each child have a day together in the course of a year.
          —*Phyllis and Merle Good, Kate and Rebecca*
          Lancaster, PA

❧   Some years ago Dad worked at a small control tower which had very little activity on the mid-watch. He took the childen along one at a time on a midnight watch, allowing them to see what he had to do and to be alone with him. They still say that meant a lot to them.
—*Rachel Tamm, Allentown, PA*

❧   For our six-year-old daughter who is deaf, we write about the day's activities in a special notebook each evening before bedtime. She needs the extra language and one-on-one attention. We now have four years' worth of "diaries" that she enjoys reviewing.
—*Roger and Pamela Rutt, Lancaster, PA*

❧   When the girls were little and I was busy during the day, I decided to institute "an hour with Mother" on an individual basis in the evenings. This did not happen very often, so it remained a special treat. On the evening for Kathie, the other two would go to bed at their regular time, but Kathie could stay up and we would do whatever she most wanted to do (within limits, of course). It might be making candy or popcorn, doing some sewing project, reading a story or whatever, but it was just for her and me. Carol and Jeanie each had their turns as well. This did not require a great deal of time, but brought pleasure and a sense of belonging and importance to each girl.
—*Miriam L. Weaver, Harrisonburg, VA*

❧   Having "art class" with a child has been a great success in our family. Adult and child begin with any size paper. Directions are given simply and slowly at first, until your child becomes familiar with this exercise. "Class" could begin something like this: (1) Make three circles anywhere on your paper. (2) Draw a line through one of the circles. (3) Fill in one of the circles with a marker. (4) Make a line beginning at the top of your paper down to the bottom. (5) Now make a dot anywhere on that line. Continue as desired. Directions should match your child's level.

It's very important to stop when your child loses interest. More important is to give your child a turn to be "in charge" and give directions. It gives them "leadership" over an adult in a positive setting. It also gives them a chance to make choices and decisions.

P.S. You are not to be "drawing" anything in particular but just having fun. Papers will be quite different even though both followed the same directions!
— *Lois and Randy Zook, Lancaster, PA*

✿ Before bedtime, our children like to read. We often pull out a book, lie down beside them, and read, too.
— *Jane-Ellen and Gerry Grunau, Winnipeg, MB*

✿ John takes one child with him to his office for an hour or so each week. They take along "quiet play" and enjoy being a part of his life at work. Our children consider this a special treat and are on their best behavior.
— *John and Ruth Miller Roth, Sarah, Leah, Hannah and Mary, Goshen, IN*

✿ Take a child along on shorter or longer trips, even if it is a business trip. It may mean extra bother and make you more inefficient, but it is easily worth the investment. Children remember these times for the rest of their lives.
— *David and Louisa Mow, Farmington, PA*

❧   Dad travels as part of his work and, usually once a year, takes one of the children with him for a few days on one of his trips. (He often chooses conferences in Seattle where an uncle, aunt, and cousins live.) As the children have gotten older, they've gained a growing understanding of what he does on his trips away.
   —*Elizabeth Loux and Don Kraybill, Matthew, Micah, and Ashley, Harleysville, PA*

❧   When each of our children were born, I wrote "A letter to my son/daughter," telling them the details surrounding their birth. I tried to be specific, without being too graphic. I expressed how much we wanted them, how we loved them even before they were born, and how precious it was to count their tiny fingers and toes. And of course I added the funny things like when Daddy ran up over an eight-inch curb trying to park in the hospital parking lot or when our daughter talked non-stop for an hour when she first held her brother. It has preserved their birth days much more than my memory ever could have!
   —*Miles and Dawnell Yoder, Lancaster, PA*

❧   Every August each child got his/her own special day to go school shopping with Mom. It always included lunch at a restaurant of his/her choice and lots of time to talk about the coming school year.
   —*Larry and Evie Hershey, Atglen, PA*

❧   For a Senior Project Lisa chose to make a crazy quilt. We shopped all over Los Angeles together to find antique fabrics, wrote to her great-aunts and grandmothers for samples, researched quilting and various stitches. It took all the hours the school allotted to the project (6 weeks) and Mom's help.
   —*Frieda Barkman, Twentynine Palms, CA*

8.
Keeping Children Creatively Occupied

❀ Painting with water on a sidewalk porch has been a great activity for our preschool-aged son.
—*Jim and Carol Spicher, Mountville, PA*

❀ Our son walked at an early age and could be destructive when we visited in homes which were not child-proofed. Our friends assured us that "He can't hurt a thing," while he proceeded to wreck things with his curiosity. We partially solved the problem by supplying him with construction blocks and puzzles which were of high interest to him. He was permitted to use them only when we were "company" and visiting away from home. To this day we refer to them as the "company" blocks.
—*John and Trula Zimmerly, Jackson, OH*

❧   We encouraged our children's grandparents to give them gifts of books, paper, glue, crayons, and tape. This supplied the children, when they were in early elementary school and younger, with endless hours of fun. Out of all the gifts they've received, their "cut stuff" was the most celebrated. We let them put on art shows—displaying their work or giving it to someone special. We let them make a mess. They also often moved half their bedroom into the living room to play house, but it was quickly cleaned up afterwards.
     —*Ellen Herr Vogts, Newton, KS*

❧   Our children are responsible for making all birthday cards which go out from our family.
     —*Jane-Ellen and Gerry Grunau, Winnipeg, MB*

❧   When the children were small, but no longer taking naps, we regularly had an hour of quiet time after lunch. Each child could look at books or read or do a quiet activity in a room by him- or herself. This gave everyone a rest. It was an especially useful practice during the summer when there were few routines.
     —*Stan and Susan Godshall, Mt. Joy, PA*

❧   I decided early on in my parenting that I wouldn't make myself indispensable to our children's play. I'd encourage creativity, but I would not entertain them all day, every day. Perhaps I accomplished this by accepting the mess creative play entails; messes were cleaned up, but during play the mess was acceptable. Clutter, rather than order and boredom.
     One year I invited all of our neighborhood children to attend an Art Show at our house. Each child was invited to bring a piece of original artwork—drawing, clay, anything. All art was displayed and easily seen—on the clothesline and on tables. After viewing together, each child was given a homemade award of some sort. No one was left out of the awards

ceremony. Then we served simple refreshments. Why didn't I make this Art Show an annual affair? Perhaps I didn't realize the lasting influence and fun of such events. Perhaps it took too much time and energy at that time in my life!
—*Charlotte H. Croyle, Archbold, OH*

✿   I feel it is important to teach our children to like themselves and to know how to be alone. We have replaced afternoon naps with an hour of quiet time now that they are older. (We do this during the summer months.) The children retreat to their rooms or to another quiet place to read, rest, or play quietly, alone. They don't complain about this, and sometimes it lasts longer than an hour.
—*Jim and Nancy Roynon, Brad, Taryn, Drew and Colin, Archbold, OH*

✿   Battery-operated toys are outlawed in our home (a few have slipped in over the years). Birthday and Christmas gifts always include basic, but hopefully somewhat unique, items such as neon paper, markers or colored pencils, chalk, cutting tools, and how-to books (origami, drawing cartoons/animals, pressing flowers, etc.).

We try to limit our children to one outside involvement of their choice, besides music lessons or choir.

Both of us are firm believers in the importance of children entertaining themselves. Because we live on a farm that we own in common with five other families, there is always something to do with 13 children around. We have lots of sports equipment (tetherball, badminton, volleyball) and encourage the children to initiate games, creek and pond fun, and general free play. One of the major reasons for the existence of our farm partnership is to establish a healthy environment for our children and their friends. We encourage our children to bring friends to our home.
—*Gretchen Hostetter Maust and Robert Maust Keezletown, VA*

✿   We had old school desks in the attic for coloring and reading on rainy days. There was also a mini-schoolroom set up in the basement with desks and chalkboard.
—*Richard and Betty Pellman, Millersville, PA*

✿   Our sons played with large furniture packing boxes. One Halloween the boys made a haunted house in our basement with boxes. They put two or three boxes in a T-formation. Children crawled in one end and brushed against rubber gloves painted red and filled with water. There were holes in the boxes where our sons could reach in and grab kids, and make weird sounds to scare them. They had several box "stations" of scary activities. One box was a coffin with somebody in it. They charged neighborhood kids one cent admission each: a real moneymaker!

Our one daughter constantly played nurse and hospital. She made nurses' uniforms out of old sheets, and later bought an old white uniform from a local thrift shop, using her own money. She'd make many charts of the body systems and, with her sister and friends, memorized her charts and spent hours bandaging and caring for her dolls. Her favorite childhood gift was an old nurses' patient chart cover and a working stethoscope.

Our other daughter more often initiated school and library play. She and her sister spent many a dreary-outside day with books and papers spread out over our basement, making all of their personal books into a Croyle Library. Many of our books still have the library envelopes and tabs they put inside each book cover.
—*Charlotte H. Croyle, Archbold, OH*

✿ I visit thrift shops during the month of October when they bring out all their weird and exotic stuff before Halloween. From these visits we've developed a very complete and diverse dress-up closet at scant expense. There seems to be no end to the fun kids can have with wigs and interesting old clothes.

—*Laura and Steve Draper, Winfield, IA*

✿ When the children were older, and after school was out, I required each of them to houseclean their bedrooms. They'd take everything out, rearrange or add things, and usually have a good time. Each summer they each learned to do one or more new things like doing laundry, making a cake, or mowing the yard. Eventually, the older children had a lawn mowing business for a number of summers, with the help of Dad.

—*Ben and Lorraine Myers, Dillsburg, PA*

✿ Our family walks to playgrounds in parks or schoolyards. We purposely purchased a home near those places so all of us, or the children alone, could do this.

—*Richard Harris and Caprice Becker, Manhattan, KS*

✿ Make provision for them to help with what you are doing. Children will gladly fill your jars with peaches or tomatoes for a small reward. They will enjoy cleaning strawberries for a few cents per quart. They also love to hang wash on the line if you provide a line they can reach. They will do a good job of dusting so you will have time to take them miniature golfing or to see some llamas or ostriches in the community.

—*Mattie Miller, Sugarcreek, OH*

✿   In summertime we require three hours of work in each child's schedule. It can be away from home (volunteering at a hospital, helping another Mom, being a library assistant, etc.), but if there is no "outside the home" work, Mom arranges work and a record is kept on the fridge! They complain but it keeps them busy, helps Mom (although it is work to keep four constructively working), and makes them feel accomplished!
    —Bylers, Williamsport, PA

✿   We invite the boys to help when we're cooking, baking, mowing, sweeping, and cleaning.
    —Kenny and Rachel Pellman, Nathaniel and Jesse
    Lancaster, PA

✿   During their elementary school days our children began creating their own plays. When they felt ready to present one, they called aunts, uncles, cousins, and friends and invited them to come. They charged one cent each and were delighted with the income and fun of presenting their own production. They even used their toddler brother in a variety of ways and coached him to say a few lines at the appropriate time.
    —Jim and Dee Nussbaum, Kidron, OH

✿   We encourage reading, sports, music lessons, and trying to follow their interests, but we also encourage them to take risks. Our 16-year-old son discovered stunt kites and has spent hours flying them. His friend also bought one, so now they can have kite fights and chases.
    —Richard and Jewel Showalter, Irwin, OH

❧   We invite our younger grandchildren to plant our garden with us. We talk about the seeds and how they grow. Together we watch the budding of trees and flowers; we look for insects and birds and talk about how God takes care of all things.
—*Erma Kauffman, Cochranville, PA*

❧   We've always tried to allow them to be interested in what we parents are doing. Christina and Colleen paint faces at some of the art fairs I attend.
—*Harvey and Lavonne Dyck, Christina and Colleen*
Viborg, SD

❧   We have put together a long list of things to do when it seems like there is nothing to do. We work on this list from time to time and add to it. It's kept in the "Things To Do" file.
—*Chuck and Robyn Nordell, Fullerton, CA*

❧   Our son recently began collecting stones, shells, bugs, etc. Instead of just putting them away, we're setting up a "science corner" in our home. We'll add the pet turtle, the goldfish, and their plants.
—*Kelli Burkholder King and John King, Jacob Hans*
and Suzanne, Goshen, IN

❧   I've started a sing/dance play group with our five-year-old. It's not formal music lessons, but the kids have fun and are learning at the same time. Three other children join us weekly for an hour of singing children's songs, moving to music, and playing rhythm instruments.
—*Anita and Randy Landis-Eigsti, Lakewood, CO*

✿   We asked the children to take music lessons through junior high. After that they got to choose whether or not to continue.
—*Stan and Susan Godshall, Mt. Joy, PA*

✿   The summer when James and John (twins and our oldest children) were 14 years old and I worked in a hospital full-time, they kept begging for home-baked bread. I told them that I was too busy to bake bread, but they could do so if they liked. One week on my day off, I baked bread, and they watched me and asked questions. The next week on my day off, they baked bread and I watched them and gave suggestions. They baked bread each week for the rest of that summer. It did not always turn out perfectly, but the whole family felt a sense of pride and pleasure in their achievement. All of our four sons, as adults, are happy and comfortable cooking and baking. The "summer of the bread-bakers" was a creative confidence-builder.
—*Wilma Beachy Gingerich, Harrisonburg, VA*

✿   Two of our children did volunteer work in a retirement home and hospital in their early teenage years before they could be employed. It was good experience for them and helped to occupy their time.
—*Marian Bauman, Harrisonburg, VA*

✿   One summer our children, then 15, 13, 11, and nine had a weekly bake sale. Some things they baked ahead and froze, like bread and cookies. Pies required their getting up early and baking them fresh on sale day. Mother bought all the ingredients. The kids researched the cost of ingredients for each item sold, then subtracted the cost before sharing out the profits. They learned bookwork, persistence, cooperation, and how to bake, although they made very little money!
—*David and Martha Clymer, Shirleysburg, PA*

✿ We've encouraged our children taking part-time jobs in restaurants and working for farmers or on carpentry crews as soon as possible. Hard work is a good discipline.
—*Richard and Jewel Showalter, Irwin, OH*

✿ We tried to provide for our children's pet interests with animals that we could accommodate—gerbils, hamsters, hermit crabs, fish, kittens, and a puppy. In lieu of our daughter having her own horse (which we couldn't adequately handle on our one-half acre lot), she attended horse camp for several summers.
—*Ernest and Lois Hess, Lancaster, PA*

✿ When I (Merle) realized that in years to come, our daughters were likely to blame me for their not having a dog as a pet when they were growing up, I presented them with a challenge. "I'm in favor of a dog," I said. "In fact, I'm disappointed that you haven't been able to solve the probable problems so we can get a dog!" What problems? So we made a list of all the possible problems (who would feed the dog, who would clean up after the dog, where would the dog stay when we're away, etc.), and the girls came up with solutions for every problem. So we got Jorg, and we've never been sorry.
—*Phyllis and Merle Good, Kate and Rebecca Lancaster, PA*

9.
What About Television?

✿   During a recent summer when a six-year-old grandson was vacationing at our home, it was the fifth day when he suddenly left the table in the dining room, went to the doorway of the living room, and glanced all around. "You don't have a TV," he said. On visits since that time we stay involved with games, puzzles, and other activities so that TV is not our entertainer.
   —*Lois Dagen, Lancaster, PA*

✿   We did not permit TV watching right after school, because the children needed physical activity. They also had to have their homework done before they could see TV, and then they had to choose shows with discretion.
   —*Bob and Doris Ebersole, Archbold, OH*

✿   We didn't have a TV until about two years ago. The rule is one hour a day. Until recently our kids didn't know anything existed besides PBS. As they get older, I'm sure it will be an issue we'll have to deal with. My husband and I don't watch TV, except when we join the children in watching their hour. We try to watch with them.

An exception to the one-hour rule—when I cut their hair they can watch an extra PBS show. They sit still and look forward a little more to haircuts!

> —*Anita and Randy Landis-Eigsti, Lakewood, CO*

✿   Our preschool children watch one half-hour program a day: children's education programs on weekday afternoons and National Geographic on Sundays. We keep our TV upstairs in our bedroom, away from our normal day's activities. Instead of watching TV, we live with a messier house, visits from neighborhood friends, and the assumption that our children will need guidance and encouragement from us throughout the day, and our suggestions for better alternatives.

> —*John and Ruth Miller Roth, Sarah, Leah, Hannah, and*
> *Mary, Goshen, IN*

✿   The more readily accessible a TV is, the harder it is to limit its use and the more likely it will be chosen over other activities. Our small portable TV is in the bedroom closet unless we decide to watch something. Beside that, having a TV that isn't very high quality and that gets only a few channels cuts down on its invasion of our family life.

> —*Herb and Sarah Myers, Mt. Joy, PA*

✿   Our children (ages eight, six, and two) are allowed one hour of TV each day. They may choose when to watch approved shows, either in the morning after they are ready for school or in the afternoon or evening after their home-work and chores are done around the house. This elimi-nates constant begging to watch TV and permits parental control. The children have some choice and usually turn it off themselves when their hour is finished. So far they are content to watch the same shows at the same time. TV hours may not accumulate if they are not used each day. Interestingly, there are many more days they do not watch their "quota," than days they do.
    —*Roger and Pamela Rutt, Lancaster, PA*

✿   When the children were preteens, we gave each one a jar of marbles. Each marble was worth one-half hour of TV time.
    When the marbles were all gone, they had to find other things to do the rest of the week. At the beginning of the week, we discussed which programs they would watch in their allotted time.
    —*Robert and Miriam Martin, East Earl, PA*

✿   When the children were young, they earned television privileges based on time spent practicing music lessons. For every 10 minutes of practice, they could watch 30 minutes of television. From junior high through high school graduation we did not have TV, for which both children have expressed deep appreciation.
    —*Mary and Nelson Steffy, East Petersburg, PA*

✿ We purposely didn't own a TV until our oldest child turned 12. Before the purchase, each of us, children and parents, wrote guidelines which we incorporated into a single list, giving each one a sense of ownership in our understanding.

—Ernest and Lois Hess, Lancaster, PA

✿ We often watch TV as a family on Friday nights. There are several programs that the children routinely watch during the week. Our basic understanding is no more than one program per day during the school year. During the summer months, the children must "buy" one hour of TV time by first reading one hour. Quite often, after an hour of reading, they opt for playing outside with friends and TV is forgotten.

—Gretchen Hostetter Maust and Robert Maust
Keezletown, VA

✿ Television is a wonderful tool. It becomes a demon when we view it as building material. Our television is not on during the day. We select programs to watch ahead of time. The anticipation is just like looking forward to seeing a movie.

—Mark and Leone Wagner, Lititz, PA

✿ Watching TV together can be a good time for physical closeness. My daughter was feeling sorry one day for a friend of hers, because "her mom and dad didn't have time to hold her and watch TV together."

—Harvey and Lavonne Dyck, Christina and Colleen
Viborg, SD

10.
What About Chores?

✿ I've enlisted our two children, at 19 months old, to help with setting the table, wiping their high chairs, and wiping the dirt on the floor. They enjoy being given special new tasks at this early age. They help me plant seeds in the garden and dig up weeds with their own tools. They love to have their own watering cans to water the veggies.
—*Marie and Ned Geiser Harnish, Indianapolis, IN*

✿ Jacob loves to vacuum and almost daily requests the vacuum cleaner. He doesn't know it's a chore, but our floors have been cleaner with his new interest. Jesse takes care of the trash.
—*Anita and Randy Landis-Eigsti, Lakewood, CO*

✿   From three years of age on, each child is responsible for making her/his bed, getting dressed, picking up her/his room, tidying the bathroom, and being present for morning prayers. In addition, each day I set the timer for 20 minutes and we all work hard. What doesn't get done waits till the next day. Having a finite time for chores makes it more acceptable to the children.

—Miki and Tim Hill, Woodstock, MD

✿   Making a written list has always worked better for us than verbal requests. Crossing things off the list gives the worker a sense of progress, and it reduces the amount of parental reminding. It also takes some forethought and seems less like making work for work's sake.

—Stan and Susan Godshall, Mt. Joy, PA

✿   I keep small wipe-off magnetic memo boards on our refrigerator doors on which I write each morning that day's list of chores. The children may do the chores any time during the day, but they must be finished before bedtime, before watching TV, and before playing with friends.

—Roger and Pamela Rutt, Lancaster, PA

✿   I believe in lists. A list of the chores children are expected to complete on a certain day or within a certain time frame gives them freedom in choosing how and when to do those jobs. Lists give them the pleasure of crossing finished things off their lists.

Another way to get the house cleaned is to put each individual job that is part of that on a separate slip of paper. (For example, dust the living room, clean the sink and tub in the bathroom, sweep the bedroom, wash the kitchen floor.) Each person pulls a slip and does what it says. Slips are pulled till all the jobs are done and the house is cleaned.

—Herb and Sarah Myers, Mt. Joy, PA

✿   Since I work part-time, I have found it goes best if I write the children's summertime chores on a list. It takes the argument out of job assignments; the children can usually choose what part of the day to do their jobs, as long as they get them done.
—*Marian Bauman, Harrisonburg, VA*

✿   Each child got a list of Saturday chores. They liked it best if I made a treasure hunt, with each note telling them what chore to do next. There was a treasure at the end, too—usually a small treat.
—*Ellen Peachey, Harpers Ferry, WV*

✿   We kept dishwashing and drying on a rotating schedule among our five children so no one always worked with the same sibling. Ours was a blended family and some of their best "talk times" were in pairs at the kitchen sink.
—*Shirley Kirkwood, Mt. Solon, VA*

✿   I make a list with weekly cleaning chores, and the boys and I sign our initials next to the jobs we will do. Sometimes having the privilege to select first is a reward for something else, or we take turns signing, or I sign for my jobs first and the boys divide the rest of them.

I usually try to rotate the tasks so I do each chore every two or three weeks. That way I can accept less than perfect performance on the jobs. I accept an honest effort at a job as "good enough," then I clean the corners the next time around, if necessary. Of course, the boys have improved their vacuuming, dusting, and bathroom-cleaning skills over the years.
—*Nancy and Clair Sauder, Lancaster, PA*

❀   I have often helped the children get started or complete chores which were tedious, and have even worked alongside them the whole time if that seemed necessary. I tried to be sure the children overheard me telling their dad, a grandparent, or a friend about the work they had done. That often helped them be less reluctant to help next time.

—*LaVerna and Lawrence Klippenstein, Winnipeg, MB*

❀   We sit down when school begins and work out a chore schedule that we all feel is manageable and helpful to the total family. When school is out, we sit down and plan a new schedule. It has always worked. We do some swapping of chores, but we are each responsible to see that our own particular jobs are covered in some way.

—*Millard and Pris Garrett, Kimmi and Krissie*
    Lancaster, PA

❀   My mother hid pennies in places I tended to skip while dusting. She would tell me how many she hid, so if I didn't find them all I'd go over my work until I found them. I got to keep them!

—*Ruth Burkholder, Bronx, NY*

II.
What About Money?

✿   We allow our preschool children to hand money to the clerk, to teach them that what we buy is exchanged for money. We've begun giving our oldest child a quarter twice a week, contingent upon a clean room, but she doesn't seem to be very motivated to earn it regularly. She accompanies me to garage sales sometimes and spends some of her allowance, which stretches it a lot further.

—*Mary Alice and Gerald Ressler, Lititz, PA*

✿   When each of our children reached age four, we began to give them a weekly allowance, not based on work, but as deserving members of the family. We did expect them, as family members, to help with family tasks. They divided their allowances three ways—10% was for giving, 20% went into their jars labeled "saving," and 70% could be used for spending. At each birthday we increased their allowances by an established amount.

Each child used his/her spending money as he/she wished, which was sometimes difficult for us to stand back and watch. At ages four and five they usually blew all of it on gum, but by age eight they had learned to save it, with the help of comments from their older siblings, such as, "You're chewing your money away." The amount of work the child did each week varied, but I found this system more workable than paying them for each job.

—*Sue Aeschliman Groff, Kinzer, PA*

✿   When our children were too young to be without a babysitter but too old to have a babysitter, we tried this approach for short absences: the three children would be their own babysitters, and we would pay them (one-third each) what we would have paid a babysitter. If they were not cooperative, they would not be paid. Several times when we came home, one child would say, "You may pay the other two, but I didn't cooperate." This taught honesty, independence, and cooperation, while still giving them an opportunity to earn money. Eventually they all three had many babysitting opportunities from neighbors and friends.

—*H. Kenneth and Audrey J. Brubaker, York, PA*

✿   I am acquainted with one family who had the following system: before the children received their allowances, they needed to show how they had used the previous week's money. It didn't necessarily matter what they had done with it, just that they were keeping track. The children needed to review their records to see where their money was going! No records—no allowance!

The father and the young son took out a loan in the son's name (with the father as cosigner) when the boy needed to buy a lawn mower to start his mowing business. He learned all about interest and repayment schedules—and he repaid the loan in full on his own!

—*Nancy Nussbaum, Elkhart, Indiana*

❁   Our children grew up on a farm with orchards, so they had seasonal opportunity to earn money by picking fruit, packing, etc. As they grew older, some solicited their school friends to take a job in the orchard. That child was responsible for overseeing those she or he invited to work. One son built a cider press from a kit and hired neighbor children to help him run it. He was responsible to pay them, and the profits from selling cider were his. That money went into his bank account for future spending. In addition to buying a bike, he later invested in a more efficient press to earn more profits.

—*Marvin and Violet Jantzi, Medina, NY*

❁   We like to teach our daughters the importance of being self-sufficient, of learning skills which are marketable so they have the choice of earning their own living. But we've also tried to emphasize that money should serve us, rather than the other way around. So we've supported our daughters in volunteer work as well. In fact, three summers of volunteer work—gardening for a museum, working at a library and hospital—is not bad preparation for learning responsibility for future earning jobs.

—*Phyllis and Merle Good, Kate and Rebecca, Lancaster, PA*

❁   As our daughter entered junior high and her desire for "proper clothes" became a major issue—with Mom being the "bad guy" who had to say "no" a lot—we switched to giving her an allowance based on a percentage of our income. If our income was reduced or increased, she realized the effect. Together we decided what her money should be spent for. The clothing then became her issue and not a source of friction between mother and daughter. She learned to sew to help reduce her expenses.

—*Ken and Helen Nafziger, Jeremy, Kirsten, and Zachary Harrisonburg, VA*

❀   When our girls were in middle school and desperately wanted brand-name clothing, we gave them the cash value of good clothing at reasonable prices. They needed to use their own money to supplement it in order to get the brand they wanted.
  —*Ken and Eloise Plank, Hagerstown, MD*

❀   When we were on vacation, we gave the kids a supply of money to cover their gift and junk-food spending, so they would not beg for money at every turn. The amount was negotiated at the start of each day when they were small, and at the beginning of the trip as they got older.
  —*Irvin and Leona Peters, Winkler, MB*

❀   We model giving by letting our children see the checks we give in the offering. We give above budget and above tithe to special funds and talk to our children about why we do it. We expect them to tithe (10%) both their allowances and paychecks.
  —*Shirley and Stuart Showalter, Goshen, IN*

12.
Cultivating Faith

✿ We allow lots of questions about faith; we discuss issues such as abortion, killing, and ethics. We still struggle with not making things too black and white for them. We see lots of "gray" in life, and we don't use religion as a fix. Passing on the faith is a challenge. I try not to preach, but share my own faith struggles. Very few of our children's peers are Christians, so we assure them that our prayers follow them daily, and that the "Hound of Heaven" follows them everywhere and will never leave them. It's our understanding of giving them back, spiritually, to God.
 —*Marvin and Rachel Miller, Indianapolis, IN*

✿ I believe in the "teachable" moment, and I believe every single day is peppered with these moments. It is my belief and hope that if we can connect faith to life's ordinary moments, we will integrate natural faith-building with life so that it becomes the children's livable faith.
 —*Mark and Leone Wagner, Lititz, PA*

❁ We like to say "God bless you" to each other. It seems more meaningful than a simple good-bye.

—*Phyllis and Merle Good, Kate and Rebecca, Lancaster, PA*

❁ It has always been the custom at our evening dinner table to have all members of their family share the experiences of their day. During their elementary and high school years our children asked many questions: "Why do we do it this way?" "What do we believe about this and why?" These questions often extended into hour-long discussions arising out of our daily happenings.

We made a major effort not to hand the children simple, pat answers which they would later feel they had to reject because they didn't make sense. We tried to be honest about our own questions and faith struggles. Our children came to see that a faith that has not been questioned is a faith not worth holding. In turn, they developed the courage to ask questions within a church community that itself was struggling to be faithful to the God in whom we place our trust.

—*Wilma Beachy Gingerich, Harrisonburg, VA*

❁ We have tried to de-emphasize the academic rat race by suggesting that, while we should all do our best in life, grades aren't everything. Accordingly, our girls know that we as parents always go to conferences with their schoolteachers with one question at the top of the list—"Do you have suggestions on how our child can grow in her respect for others, even if her report card doesn't measure that?"

—*Phyllis and Merle Good, Kate and Rebecca, Lancaster, PA*

✿   We are expecting our third child. As a family we are praying daily for the baby. Everyone lays their hand "on the baby," and one, two, three, or all of us pray. This has helped our children express their fears about the baby and to share in the nurturing of the unborn child. It was the kids' idea to add a kiss after the prayer.
    —*Ellen Herr Vogts, Newton, KS*

✿   During the summer, our best intentions and attempts fall apart as the madness of the peaches, blueberries, tomatoes, and grapes is upon us. (We are fruit and vegetable farmers!) But our usual practices are, at the beginning of each month, to all help to choose songs, one for each day of the week, which we sing for prayer at our evening meal as we join hands around our table. Following this we have a moment of quiet, which is open for anyone to offer audible prayer. During our meal, one parent reads a short selection from a devotional book, which we follow with conversation on the reading, or on the day's activities, or on just about anything.
    We have found this to be good family time as we gather for a moment of togetherness in our usually busy day.
    —*Samuel C. and Margaret Wenger Johnson, Bart and Hannah, Keezletown, VA*

✿   When our four sons were ages six to 13, the older two were absorbed in world history and geography in school. We decided to tap into this interest by using selected segments of the Macmillan Bible Atlas in our family devotions. We read an Atlas entry each evening, followed by Bible passages which provided the context for that particular entry. We then discussed the historical, social setting in which the story took place. Together we would imaginatively seek to reconstruct the event. The 13- and nine-year-olds were interested and excited by this activity. But the enthusiasm of the older ones did not always bring the six-year-old along.

So we alternated with several months of stories on a level which held his interest. But in the process, the imaginative reconstruction of the faith story took root.

> —*Wilma Beachy Gingerich, Harrisonburg, VA*

✿ Most of our times of worship and prayer come from a continuous attitude that acknowledges God's presence and power in our lives. If the news has stories that need prayer, we stop and pray. If we hear a siren, we stop and pray for God's protection or comfort for whatever is going on.

> —*Chuck and Robyn Nordell, Fullerton, CA*

✿ Our intention in raising our family in a mixed neighborhood in the center city has been to introduce our daughters to the variety of economic classes and races in the human family, as well as learning to live with limited space and resources.

> —*Phyllis and Merle Good, Kate and Rebecca*
> *Lancaster, PA*

✿ We pray together at special moments on our travels or pause to pray at the edge of our newly planted garden. We've tried to emphasize the spontaneous occasions for cultivating faith.

> —*Ernest and Lois Hess, Lancaster, PA*

✿ We cultivate our children's faith by faithfully attending church on Sundays and also Wednesday evenings. We have started to have a catered dinner in our congregation on Wednesday nights (you can come anytime from 5:30 to 6:30 to eat); then at 7:00 there are Clubs, MYF, or Bible Studies for all ages. It's been a wonderful experience for our children to see and interact with church friends more than just on Sunday mornings.

> —*Mike and Kim Pellman, Matt and Brooke*
> *Bird-in-Hand, PA*

❁   Since our house church groups are small, we have replaced children's Sunday school with intergenerational activities. We may have a drama or activities center to stimulate thinking. The dramas are very simple and basic. We often rehearse them only once or twice prior to the service.

We have a Teen Entry Celebration when a young person joins the church. The event is planned by the individual youth, parents, and the youth leader, and usually reflects the special interests of the child. Our son, for example, who is interested in sports, had a focus on the biblical virtues which can be developed and strengthened through sports.

—*Glennis and Mark Yantzi, Kitchener, ON*

❁   Every person in your congregation from first grade through college (and older!) should have a specific job to do. This could be making a banner once or twice a year, passing the offering plate, helping with children's time, rearranging furniture during the service, holding roving microphones when you have special guests, helping in the nursery or toddler room, making something special for fellowship meals, making Advent candles each year, illustrating the cover of your newsletter, reviewing children's books for the newsletter, reading Scripture, managing the overhead projector during singing, signing for the deaf, helping count the offering, etc.

—*Nancy Nussbaum, Elkhart, IN*

❁   We have a hymn-singing evening at our house for friends on Friday or Saturday nights.

—*Christine Certain, Fresno, CA*

❁   We had bedtime Bible stories every night. Our daughter now gives a copy of the book we read from as a baby shower gift to her friends.

—*Jim and Shirley Hershey, Bloomingdale, NJ*

I3.
Family Vacations

✿ On long trips we took along little packages (number determined by the length of the trip) to be opened at intervals, also based on the length of the trip. These packages included such things as gum, a new book to look at or read, a game to play, magic tablets that revealed a picture when scribbled over with a pencil, etc. Singing rounds, playing 20 Questions, or telling continued stories became more popular as the girls got older.

—*Herb and Sarah Myers, Mt. Joy, PA*

✿ While traveling, we rotated where each person sat. And we took along cookie sheets and playdough. We also had a "surprise" box. Each day they received a small gift that could be used on the trip.

—*Bob and Doris Ebersole, Archbold, OH*

❀　Our one daytime travel pastime was finding A-Z letters on billboards, signs, trucks, etc. (It was while playing this game, we discovered our third grade daughter needed glasses. She couldn't see letters at a distance like the rest of us could.) Our other most used card game was Crow. Each card had a picture of an object like a bicycle, clock, girl walking, railroad track, policeman, school bus, cow, bird flying, etc. When the item on the card was actually spotted out the window, the person with that card would say "Caw, Caw." We continued playing until all the items were seen.

—*Lois Dagen, Lancaster, PA*

❀　Players count certain animals on the side of the road closest to them (dogs, cows, horses), only one category at a time. The first side to reach 25 wins. Passing a cemetery cancels the count on the side of the road on which it appeared.

Add interest by assigning different numerical values to cows, horses, tractors, or cemeteries.

—*Orpah and Elam Kurtz, Jefferson, NC*

❀　To play Ghost, the first player begins spelling a word by giving its first letter (but not disclosing what the word is). Each succeeding player adds a letter to continue building a word, but also trying to make the next player end the word. The player who has to end a word takes the first letter of the word GHOST. Each time someone ends a word she/he takes on an additional letter of GHOST until she/he has fully spelled the word GHOST. At that point, the player who has completed GHOST drops out of active play and sits there silently, listening like a GHOST! Play continues until all but one player become GHOSTS.

—*Laura and Steve Draper, Winfield, IA*

❁ One game for riding in the car involves looking for objects or places on a list prepared ahead of time by parents. The first one to find all the things on the list earns points.
—*Richard and Betty Pellman, Millersville, PA*

❁ On long trips each person gets an opportunity to choose one fast-food place to eat. We watch for letters of the alphabet in road signs and license plates to spell each member of the family's name. Other adaptations can be improvised; the town and state where you live, each person's birthdate, etc.
—*Anna Yoder, Millersburg, OH*

❁ We exchange toys with friends so that the children have toys which are new to them for the trip.
—*Bob and Jeanne Horst, Harrisonburg, VA*

❁ We listened to music during long hours in the car—the parents supplied one tape of music, and then the kids supplied the next tape. Neither party could complain about the music. The kids learned to appreciate classical music; the parents learned a lot about and came to appreciate much of the kids' music. All of our musical horizons widened!
—*Irvin and Leona Peters, Winkler, MB*

❁ When our children were younger, we did lots and lots of singing in the car, leaving out words that they filled in.
—*Mark and Leone Wagner, Lititz, PA*

❁ We do cross-stitch and needlepoint in the car.
—*Tom and Lois Marshall, Spruce, MI*

❀ During long car trips we always stop for a "get physical" session at a roadside park.
—*Jenny and Dave Moser, Bluffton, OH*

❀ We play the "family guessing game" while driving. One person chooses a family we all know. The rest of us may ask yes or no questions to try to guess which family has been selected. When we guess the right one, it becomes someone else's turn.
—*Kenny and Rachel Pellman, Nathaniel and Jesse*
Lancaster, PA

❀ Before one 20-hour trip we made an idea box that everyone was requested to contribute to. No one else was allowed to read the ideas until we were actually traveling. Then when people started getting scrappy we pulled out an idea. Everyone had made an agreement that everyone would participate, whether they felt like it or not. Ideas ranged wide—singing, reading aloud, arm wrestling, finger wrestling, Who Am I? (guess by yes or no answers), standing on your head while staying in your seatbelt, etc.
—*David and Martha Clymer, Shirleysburg, PA*

❀ A favorite game that we frequently played is a word game called "On the Whole or Beheaded." "It" thinks of a word that becomes a different word when its first letter is removed ("Beheaded"). "It" then gives hints for both words and the other players try to guess. ("On the whole" I'm thinking of a word that is part of your house—wall; "Beheaded," it means everything—all. Or "On the whole" I'm thinking of a large animal—bear. "Beheaded," it's part of your body—ear.)
—*Mary and Nelson Steffy, East Petersburg, PA*

✿   Traveling with binoculars is a lot of fun.
      —*Edwin Miller, Wellman, IA*

✿   We start long trips at 2-3:00 in the morning, so that
when the children wake up we are halfway there!
      —*Mary Hochstedler and Ruth Andrews, Kokomo, IN*

✿   While we waited during a two-hour layover at an air-
port last summer, a bottle of bubbles entertained our
one-and-a-half-year-old for quite a while!
      —*Brenda Augsburger Yoder, Lancaster, PA*

✿   When the boys were little, and even now, it helped(s)
to tell how long the day's travels are expected to take. "We
should be there by supper time" helped to avoid a lot of
impatient questions. Our younger son always traveled much
better if he knew what type of sleeping arrangement he was
headed for—a motel, someone's house, etc.
      —*Nancy and Clair Sauder, Lancaster, PA*

✿   On long trips (four-plus hours) we give each child a
coin purse with 20 dimes. Each time there is griping, teas-
ing, picking, or other behavior unacceptable to a parent, a
dime fine is charged to one or both children and is put in
the parking meter drawer (sometimes called an ashtray).
When we reach our destination, the children get to keep the
remaining money—usually $1.90. It is amazing how the car
atmosphere has changed. They actually discuss disagree-
ments amicably and resist urges to pick and complain. If
they argue with me when the fine is levied, I double it.
      —*Gretchen Hostetter Maust and Robert Maust*
       Keezletown, VA

✿   While traveling we tried to stop at our campground early enough in the day so the children would have time to play before supper and bedtime.
—*Ken and June Weaver, Harrisonburg, VA*

✿   My husband learned his leisurely style of vacationing from his family. They always left plenty of time to explore things that were not on their original itinerary. By practicing this together we have enjoyed lively county fairs, witnessed spectacular sunsets, discovered petting zoos and new museums, and learned a great deal of history and folklore from roadside markers. Done this way, getting there really is half the fun.
—*Kristine Griswold, Falls Church, VA*

✿   When children are smaller, it's much easier to go to one place and stay there, rather than traveling constantly. We find camping or renting a cottage is one of our favorite activities. The water is a natural and excellent entertainer of children, be it a lovely beach somewhere or the ocean. A shovel and bucket are the only toys you need.
—*Elizabeth Weaver, Thorndale, ON*

✿   We enjoyed house-sitting for our children's grandparents, who lived in another area, so they could "get lost" together, and so our children could explore and become acquainted with an area where one parent grew up.
—*Richard and Betty Pellman, Millersville, PA*

✿   At the beginning of the summer we make a summer jar of "day trips." Sundays are especially good days to pull a slip out of the jar and enjoy a quick "surprise" trip. Favorite repeats each year were collecting a variety of leaves at a local state park and following a nearby creek.
—*Janice Miller and David Polley, Ann Arbor, MI*

✿ Some vacations are reserved for "mystery" trips of two or three days. Each member gets one choice of a place to go, but does not tell the rest of the family. Children who do not drive share the secret with one parent, so that parent knows where to drive and make reservations as necessary. This exposes children older than seven to some of the responsibilities of planning. As preparations are made, all persons are informed concerning special items to pack. Children and adults attempt to solve the mystery of where they are going. This promotes awareness of geography and of local places of interests.

—*Anna Yoder, Millersburg, OH*

✿ On long trips with preschoolers, we ate lunch in the car while driving. Then we stopped at a park to play. After being in the car, the children were not interested in sitting in a restaurant.

—*The Baker-Smiths, Stanfield, OR*

14.
Creating a
Sense of Family

❀   When my farmer husband is working in the fields, we pack a supper and all go out to eat with him. I make it a priority to rearrange schedules so we can all eat together.
   —*Joan and Jim Ranck, Christiana, PA*

❀   Our two married daughters live within five miles of us. They and their mother work full-time. More than two years ago, they decided to take turns cooking supper. On Monday, Sarah cooks enough for everyone. The girls or their spouses stop by for their share. Tuesday and Wednesday they take their turns cooking. Friday and Saturday we eat leftovers or go out to eat. We believe it's more economical this way, and the cooks have learned it's easier.
   —*Leroy and Sarah Miller, Chesapeake, VA*

❀   In an effort to create a sense of global family, we prepare a meal from another country once a month. After we

eat together, we read about the country and find it on a map of the world.
　—*Wayne and Mary Nitzsche, Wooster, OH*

✿　We tried to eat at least one meal together each day, usually in the evening. Sometimes we would play the game, "Trading Characters," at these meals. To trade characters, two persons simply exchange their regular places at the table (Son sits where Dad usually sits and Dad sits where Son usually sits). Then each person tries to act like the character who usually sits in that place. We found this to be quite revealing about how parents are perceived by children, and vice versa. We always did this in fun and with some exaggeration. We learned a lot!
　—*Glen and Thelma Horner, Morton, IL*

✿　We say no to Sunday evening activities. We keep that as a family time, so we can regroup before beginning a new week.
　—*Mark and Leone Wagner, Lititz, PA*

✿　On days when I am home, the children and I "hit" the sofa in the living room after school and sit together to talk about the day—theirs and mine. I think it's important to tell them about the good and bad things which happened in my day, so they will learn the "two-way-ness" of communication in a family.
　—*Jane-Ellen and Gerry Grunau, Winnipeg, MB*

✿　We enlist technology to protect us from technology—in the form of an answering machine. When the phone rings during supper, bedtime stories, or other special times, we let the machine pick up the call. (Since Ann is a pastor there are lots of calls.)
　—*Ann Becker and Byron Weber, Kitchener, ON*

✿   We talk openly about everything. We share our feelings, concerns, and solutions. The kids know they are deeply loved, even though we have our share of battles of the wills. We do silly things, act silly—and generally enjoy life. I volunteer once a week at a nursing home, and I am reminded weekly about how short life is.

—Patrick and Gina Glennon, Carolyn and Steven
Turnersville, NJ

✿   Be sure to get everyone away from civilization together—it's especially important with teens—or from anyone who might know us, for at least a few days. That creates special memories and "in-family" jokes.

Backpacking together is great. Camping out. Long trips in the car! Eating supper in Daddy's office lounge when he can't come home! Having subs or pizza (special deals in our town) the day Mom works and gets home late! We hold family conferences where we plan at least a once-a-month special experience. The treasurer keeps track of budget—one month may be free tubing in the creek and one month cross-country skiing for just our family.

—Bylers, Williamsport, PA

✿   When one child is invited away, the one staying home gets special attention. Staying home alone with parents can be as much fun as going away. We have food chosen by the child, and we may watch a video together or go somewhere special.

—Kenny and Rachel Pellman, Nathaniel and Jesse
Lancaster, PA

✿   To give our children a sense of family, we sometimes shared private matters which we called "family secrets." They proved to be trustworthy at those times and were rewarded with some sort of celebration, such as going out for dinner to a special place, for example, when we cleared the mortgage!

—Richard and Betty Pellman, Millersville, PA

✿   When I was a child, my dad, who was a minister and bishop, had frequent speaking engagements—especially on weekends. The rare Sunday evenings that he had free were special times for the entire family. A special event on such a Sunday night was when Dad took his reel-to-reel tape recorder into the parlor, that special room entered only on special occasions, and, beginning with the youngest family member, interviewed us—individually. We would all sit with Mother in Dad's study as she monitored the traffic flow and told the next family member when it was his/her time to enter the parlor for a private minute with Dad. The suspense and anticipation were almost unbearable! The questions from Dad were different for each member of the family, and were always directed to something pertinent or relevant in our experience.

Then after all the children were hosted, Mother and Dad had a few minutes to talk by themselves. They then called all of us back into the parlor, and we listened as Dad played back the interviews. The baby (and there was always one or two, it seemed) would utter little more than a "da-da" or coo, and we were delighted. Some would sing a song. When all the children were through, Mother and Dad would come on, telling us what wonderful children we were and how grateful they were to be our parents. Then Dad would say, "It's been a long day and since you were good boys and girls, Mother has a popsicle for each of you," and would assign a family member to go to the cellar and get them from the locker. It was always a wonderful surprise because we had no idea there were any popsicles on the premises. It all ended too quickly.

—Melvin Thomas, Lancaster, PA

✿   We have a master calendar where we put everyone's activities. Each person has a different colored felt pen. Because of our business, evenings at home and days with nothing scheduled are precious to us as parents, and this has rubbed off on our children.

   —*Jim and Nancy Roynon, Brad, Taryn, Drew, and Colin*
     Archbold, OH

✿   I believe one of the most important strengths in our family is a sense of humor and fun. Our girls even comment now, as they visit friends' homes, that we have fun together. It's not that we do anything special; it's just an attitude of being able to laugh at ourselves and situations. Often it helps the girls do chores and things that they don't care to do—through finding the humor.

   —*Harvey and Lavonne Dyck, Christina and Colleen*
     Viborg, SD

✿   We've started a Christmas gift tradition where, instead of giving things, we give time gifts to parents. We just finished one such weekend at a cabin—we plan the time, prepare the food, and provide the space. It allows an extended time together to play, visit, and have fun. We've created some great memories.

   —*Kenny and Rachel Pellman, Nathaniel and Jesse*
     Lancaster, PA

✿   We usually keep Friday night open for a family activity. It may involve games at home, going out for pizza, shopping for clothes, or an occasional game of miniature golf or bowling. Sometimes our family activity is with another family, but usually we spend the time as an immediate family unit.

   —*Nancy and Clair Sauder, Lancaster, PA*

✿   We schedule what we call "Family Meetings" as needed. We reserve at least a half hour, and we all sit down
together in our family room. These meetings often focus on
a problem we're experiencing as a family, but which doesn't
have a ready solution. By making an event of the meeting,
the problem gets special attention, and, more often than
not, the girls are the ones who come up with the solution!
Examples: making mealtime less fragmented, setting bedtime, settling arguments, deciding on clothing allowance,
making chores more fair. We have several rules for these
meetings: no phone calls, no one leaves until a decision is
made, and everyone must try to listen to the others.

—*Phyllis and Merle Good, Kate and Rebecca, Lancaster, PA*

About the Authors

Phyllis Pellman Good and Merle Good have teamed together on a variety of projects, beginning in the early 1970s with an experimental theater.

Today, they jointly oversee the operation of The People's Place, a heritage interpretation center abut the Amish and Mennonites, in Intercourse, Pennsylvania, a village in eastern Lancaster County. They also operate The Old Country Store and several other shops located nearby.

Merle Good is the publisher of Good Books and Phyllis Pellman Good is Book Editor. Together and individually they have written numerous books and articles.

The Goods live in the city of Lancaster with their two daughters.